S

RED YESTERDAYS

Also by Glenn Shirley

The Life of Texas Jack
Shotgun For Hire
Buckskin Joe
Henry Starr, Last of the Real Badmen
Born To Kill
Heck Thomas, Frontier Marshal
Outlaw Queen
Buckskin and Spurs
Pawnee Bill
Law West of Fort Smith
Six-Gun and Silver Star
Toughest of Them All

RED YESTERDAYS

By

Glenn Shirley

For permission to reprint and adapt certain
chapters and parts of chapters included in this
book, the author wishes to thank Western Publi-
cations, Inc., of Austin, Texas (1); Major Maga-
zines, Inc., of New York (2); *Real West* magazine,
of Derby, Connecticut (3, 7, 10, 11, 13); Stagecoach Publishing Company, of New York (4, 8);
and *Westerner* magazine of Encino, California
(5, 6, 9, 12, 14).

v

CONTENTS

Book Five

SILVER STARS AND SUDDEN GUNS

Book Six

WHEELS TO SUNDOWN

FOREWORD

People, more than events and places, make history interesting. The blend of primitive Folsom man and Spanish, French and British explorers with a startling variety of Indian tribes, the outlaws and lawmen, the cowboy, Boomer, and the homesteaders that followed, bringing their politics, religion, their customs and lore, made the history of the vast section of the southwest known as Indian Territory the most fascinating and diverse of any other American dimension.

During the first half of the nineteenth century, Indian Territory became the residence of the Five Civilized Tribes by the process of removal, as a policy of the United States government. After the Civil War, the occupancy of these Five Nations was reduced roughly to the eastern half of the region, with the small tribes of the Quapaw Agency as neighbors to the northeast, and the Osages and Plains tribes located in the western half on reservations. The steady drift of whites into the Nations, doubling within a decade the population in the eastern half, brought eventual doom to the Indian governments. As the reservations on the west were dissolved and opened to homestead settlement by a series of "runs," drawings and lot auctions to the highest bidders, the denizens of all civilization came in all tongues and garb and every imaginable odor. By 1907, this heterogenous aggregation had welded itself into the state of Oklahoma.

Describing in one volume the event-filled rise of Indian Territory as the 46th Star might satisfy the general reader, but would leave the more serious student somewhat less than satisfied. On the other hand, there are certain advantages in having individuals personify important periods of history. Stories of individuals have narrative as well as educative values, and consolidating the deeds of these earnest, energetic people in single persons will better serve to extol the complexities and diversities of this vast drama in the brief space here.

Nor has an effort been made to deal with the exploits and heroic legends of its well-known men and women. While the characters selected did not prosper or guide the destiny of the territory so much as other better-touted participants, their activities are nonetheless equal in daring and excitement. Of the good and bad, of the admirable and contemptible, they had one thing in common—they gave the period life and color. Many of them achieved national and even international fame. More importantly, they perhaps better represent cross-segments of Oklahoma's red yesterdays that were, and in this bicentennial year should be remembered.

Glenn Shirley

On the Cimarron
Payne County, Oklahoma
1976

RED YESTERDAYS

OUR WILD INDIANS

BOOK 1

"My red brethren just like wild ones
(Kiowas and Comanches). They say to
United States, "Here my war hatchet;
no more war,' then break treaty . . . .
We all want peace among ourselves
and with United States. We want our
country; we love it all here together."

—Black Beaver

1. Abe Lincoln of the Delawares

The Lenni-Lenape, or Delaware, Indians have always claimed to be the grandfathers of all other red men. At the time of the first white settlements on the Atlantic coast, these Indians formed the most important confederacy of the Algonquin-speaking tribe and occupied a large area of present Delaware, New Jersey, New York and Pennsylvania.

Benjamin West's famous painting depicts William Penn, the founder of Pennsylvania, making a treaty with their leading warriors and great chief, Tamenend, under an immense spreading elm at Shackamaxon, on the banks of the Delaware River, in October, 1682. This treaty, said to have been the only one not sworn to, was never broken. Due to Penn's sagacious recognition of Indian titles and buying land instead of seizing, the Delawares did not avenge the white encroachments by massacres. In the early 1700s they began their movement westward in hope of preserving their way of life. By 1751 they had settled in eastern Ohio, where they remained until forced into Indiana and later Illinois. In 1818 they ceded all their lands east of the Mississippi and moved to the James Fork of White River in Missouri. Some went to the Red River on the Texas border, by Spanish permission. By 1835 the main body of the tribe had been gathered on a reservation on the Kansas River near Fort Leavenworth and remained there until transferred after the Civil War to the Cherokee Nation. Today the great majority of their remaining members live in Washington, Nowata and Craig counties, Oklahoma, and have wisely invested their funds in homes and farm improvements.

But the main reason for their feeling of superiority is that one of their leaders was the famed guide and interpreter Black Beaver.

3

This Indian, Black Beaver, was an anomaly of his race and time. His melancholy eyes, high bones over hollowed cheeks, sensitive mouth, large nose and unruly hair resembled the beardless Abraham Lincoln. He was born three years before the Great Emancipator, in 1806, on the site of present Belleville, while his people still occupied the beautiful bluffs on the Illinois side of the Mississippi.

His parents named him "Se-ket-Tu-May-Qua" (also spelled "Si-ki-to-ker"). By the time the tribe moved to Missouri, he was old enough to join the fur trappers and river men streaming in and out of St. Louis, and his name had been anglicized to Black Beaver.

Over the next fifty years he would see almost every mountain range and river to the West and help bring fame to many of the great military and scientific explorers. Colonel Randolph B. Marcy, in his book *Thirty Years of Army Life On the Border* (1866), gives the first accounts of his exploits.

In the 1830s, when John Jacob Astor's American Fur Company was extending its activities into the central Rocky Mountain region, Black Beaver accompanied twenty white men and four Delawares to one of the trading posts on the Upper Missouri to trap beaver. While at the stockade fort, the party was attacked by a large band of Blackfeet, determined to destroy the post.

When it appeared there was no probability of the attacking party abandoning its purpose, "one damned fool Delaware," as Beaver put it, proposed that the defenders make a sortie upon the Blackfeet. Beaver, who had never been in battle, began trembling so badly he could hardly stand.

He had left home, however, with the avowed intention of becoming a distinguished brave. With great effort he stifled his emotions. "Why, it

4

is just the idea I was about to suggest!" he replied. And, slapping his comrade on the back, he charged through the gate, yelling at the others to follow.

They had advanced only a short distance when a shower of arrows fell upon them. Luckily, no one was wounded. His companions proposed a retreat, and Beaver agreed. But when he discovered the others were leaving him behind in their flight to safety, he stopped and shouted to them: "Come back, you cowards, you squaws; what for you run away and leave me fight alone?" His taunt halted the retreat. The men rallied, succeeded in beating off the enemy and saved the fort.

Afterward the captain in charge shook his hand, saying, "Beaver, you have done this day what no other man in the fort had the courage to do. I thank you from the bottom of my heart." Thus the Delaware achieved his reputation as a brave warrior.

A second test of his courage came a few weeks later. He had been left alone upon the headwaters of the Missouri in charge of a large quantity of supplies which had been buried to keep the Indians from stealing them. Beaver amused himself by hunting in the vicinity, checking the cache once a day. Arriving upon the crest of a hill on one of his visits, he found a band of Blackfeet occupying the locality and feared they might appropriate the supplies.

The hostiles spied him and signaled him down for a chat. Realizing their purpose was to take him into custody, he replied that he was not in a talking humor and started off the opposite direction. They hallooed after him, using the most insulting language and gestures, asked if he considered himself a man to run away from his friends, and intimated: "You old womans who should go home and take care of the children!"

This so aroused Beaver's indignation that he stopped, turned back, and replied, "Maybe so; s'pose three-four you come up here alone, I'll show you if I'ze old womans."

His challenge went unaccepted and the Indians rode off, leaving the cache undiscovered.

Beaver's activities the next ten years are uncertain. There is evidence that he was employed for a time as a hunter by William and Charles Bent at Bent's old fort in southeastern Colorado, and served as scout on one of Colonel John C. Fremont's early expeditions to the Pacific.

In describing this period of his life, Marcy states that

> He had visited nearly every point of interest within the limits of our unsettled territory. He had set his traps and spread his blanket on the headwaters of the Missouri and Columbia ... south to the Colorado and Gila, and thence to the shores of Southern California. His life had been that of a veritable cosmopolite, filled with scenes of intense and startling interest, bold and reckless daring . . . .

Colonel Richard Irving Dodge, who employed Black Beaver as interpreter at his treaty council with the Comanche, Kiowa and Wichita on the North Fork of Red River in 1834, lauded him for his "wonderful journeys . . . undertaken from pure curiosity and love of adventure" and a "more minute and extensive personal knowledge of the North American continent than any other man ever had or probably will have."

In 1843, he was back with the American Fur Company, headquartered at Fort Union on the Missouri. It was here that the celebrated ornithologist, painter and naturalist, John James

6

Audubon, employed him for a busy summer of collecting birds and animals. He paid from $2 for a large porcupine to $20 for a grizzly bear.

Audubon took Beaver with him on his return to Galveston, Texas. From there they were to take a ship to New York, and the next year he and Beaver would start from New York and tour the country back to the Missouri.

Beaver had never seen a ship. He studied those in port a few days, and finally asked Audubon if people ever died on board during a voyage. Audubon told him they did.

"What you do with dead?" he inquired.

Audubon replied that they were cast into the sea.

Beaver reflected a moment. "I not enter ship," he said, and Audubon lost his faithful guide.

When war was declared with Mexico, Beaver was back with his people in eastern Kansas. Somewhere in his wanderings he had met Colonel William Selby Harney of the 2nd Dragoons. Advised that Harney needed recruits, he organized a mounted company of Delawares and thirty-five of their Shawnee neighbors. They were mustered into the United States Army, with Beaver as captain, on June 1, and discharged in August, 1846.

Thomas C. Battey, a teacher among the Caddoes on the Washita and later among the Kiowas, kept a diary which he published in 1875 as *The Life and Adventures of A Quaker Among the Indians*. In this treasure house of information on these tribes, Battey states that he once asked Beaver why he, an Indian, had enlisted to fight the Mexicans, and Beaver replied: "I had seen cannon around white men's forts and could not make up my mind how soldiers fought with them big guns." But Battey knew his wry, indirect friend well enough to realize it had been a simple act of patriotism. Beaver proudly re-

7

tained his military title the rest of his life.

When Colonel Marcy first met Black Beaver in 1849, the Delaware was living with Shawnee friends at Edwards Trading Post near Shawnee-town, 125 miles west of Fort Smith, Arkansas on the Canadian River. Marcy had left Fort Smith on April 4 with eighty-four dragoons and infantrymen under orders to establish the best route to Santa Fe and escort an accompanying train of 500 California-bound goldseekers. Pausing at the post to repair equipment and purchase horses, cattle, feed and necessities not available the next several hundred miles, the noted pathfinder engaged Beaver as a guide and interpreter. Marcy noted: "He was an intelligent Indian and proved to be most useful . . . ."

As the expedition proceeded west over unmapped hills, streams and prairies, Beaver showed him where drinkable water could be found, where grass was available for horses and oxen, and pointed out types of brush cover for deer and wild turkey. One day Beaver informed him that they were passing through the last stand of hickory timber. Marcy had a supply cut sufficient to replace poles and axles for the remainder of their journey.

Beaver also kept an eye out for marauding Indians. He taught the colonel how to determine what tribe had abandoned a certain campsite from the way they had built their fires and lodges, and how many were in the party. Thus he knew whether they were friendly or hostile, and by observing the trail they had made upon leaving, if enemies, knew what direction to take to avoid them.

The grace and rapidity with which Black Beaver conversed with Indians they encountered astonished Marcy:

On June 1, having marched fourteen miles and made camp at a small lake on the high prairie, we received a visit from four Kioways, dressed in war costume and armed with rifles, bows, shields and lances. They were on their way, they told us, to Chihuahua, Mexico, to steal mules and horses. I brought them into camp and told them we were disposed to be friendly and at peace with Kioways; that it was the desire of their "great father," the President of the United States, to be on terms of peace with all his "red children." This appeared to please them, and they replied that they would communicate my "talk" to their people. I was much surprised at the ease with which Beaver communicated with them in pantomine . . . . I have no hesitation in saying he would compare with the most accomplished performers of our operas.

Having visited many of the large towns on the Missouri and Mississippi, Beaver prided himself no little upon his acquaintance with the customs of the whites and was always happiest when displaying this knowledge in the presence of Indian companions. A Comanche scout bivouacked at Beaver's fire one evening. Marcy dropped by to find the pair engaged in "earnest and not very amicable" conversation. On inquiring the cause, Beaver answered, "I've been telling this Injun what I seen 'mong white folks."

"Well," asked Marcy, "what did you tell him?"

"I tell him 'bout steamboats and railroads and heap o' houses I seen in St. Louis."

"And what does he think about that?"

"He say I'ze damned fool."

"What else did you tell him?"

"I tell him world is round, but he keep all e time say, 'Hush, you fool! do you s'pose I'ze child? Haven't I got eyes? Can't I see prairie? You call him round?' Then I tell him all the rivers he seen, all e'time the water he run; s'pose the world flat, the water he stand still. He still no b'lieve me."

Marcy said, "Why don't you explain to him the magnetic telegraph?"

Beaver looked at the colonel inquisitively. "What you call magnetic telegraph?"

"You have heard of New York and New Orleans?"

Beaver nodded.

"Well," Marcy explained, "we have a wire connecting these two cities, which are a thousand miles apart, and would take a man thirty days to ride it on a good horse. Now a man stands at one end of this wire in New York, and by touching it a few times inquires of his friend in New Orleans what he had for breakfast. His friend in New Orleans touches the other end of the wire, and in ten minutes the answer comes — 'Ham and eggs.' Tell him that, Beaver."

The Delaware stared at him incredulously. Finally he remarked: "Injun not very smart, but he holler pretty loud; you hear him maybe half a mile. You say 'Merican man talk thousand miles? No, sir, I not tell him that, for I don't believe it myself."

Beaver turned the tables a few days later.

On June 19 they encamped upon a small creek between two mountains, named by the Comanche "Big and Little Tucumcarie" (near present Tucumcari, New Mexico). The expedition had received good treatment while passing through the Comanche country, and a body of these Indians rode in to trade with the emigrants and soldiers.

The colorful spectacle made a lively impres-

10

sion on topographer Lieutenant J.H. Simpson:

> They were all mounted either on full sized American horses, mustangs, mules or ponies. Their dress generally consisted of leggings and moccasins, with a buffalo robe or hand-woven blanket about their loins, and very large rings on their arms and in their ears. Some of the more foppish young men were gorgeously decked in leggins of bright red strouding and blankets extravagantly worked with beads, and wore a cue made of buffalo hair hanging from the back of the head to the ground, garnished consecutively with circular plates beaten out from dollars. A bow clung over the shoulder, and a quiver of arrows attached to their saddle, constituted their only weapons.

The old chief, Is-sa-ki-ep, professed much love for whites and seized Marcy in his brawny arms while still on their horses, giving him a bruin-like squeeze. Marcy, "for the good of the service," forced himself to submit. He was mistaken, however, in thinking the salutation had been completed:

> Again the savage flung his arms around my shoulders, rubbing his greasy face against mine. All of which, Beaver informed me (grinning inwardly), was a signal mark of affection and his utmost expression of friendship and good will.

The Indians followed them into camp, where Marcy repeated the President's desire to be at peace with all his red children. The Indians as-

11

sured him that they loved the emigrants so much it almost broke their hearts. Marcy gave them pipes and tobacco, and they "went off well pleased."

But the fun had only begun.

Is-sa-ki-ep and about fifty braves returned to the camp next morning, with several women and children. Comanche women were, as in many other wild tribes, the slaves of their lords, and it was common practice for their husbands to lend or sell them to a visitor for two or three days at a time. The women never refused to submit. In case of disobedience, their husbands did not hesitate to punish them by cutting off an ear or a nose. Judging the specimens before him, covered with filth, their hair cut close to the head and features ugly to the extreme, Marcy thought them "the most repulsive objects of the female kind on earth."

The Indians renewed their promises of friendship, which Marcy received with a "semblance of confidence." But he was no less vigilant in the care of the livestock. He gave them an ox, which they slaughtered at once with an arrow.

The council concluded, Marcy mixed a glass of brandy toddy which he offered the chief. Is-sa-ki-ep tasted the beverage, puckered his lips, then passed it around the circle. Again he assured the colonel that the migrants would not be molested.

Afterwards, Marcy observed Black Beaver in "quite an animated conversation" with the old chief and summoned him to inquire what they were discussing. The 500 emigrants and soldiers were gathered around the circle, all ears for everything that transpired.

"He say," Beaver replied, pointing to two squaws seated nearby, "he bring you two wife."

Marcy flushed, and a titter swept through the assembly.

"Tell him," the colonel said, recovering from

his embarrassment, "that this is not in accordance with the customs of the white people; that they only have one wife at home, and are not disposed to marry others abroad."

Beaver interpreted this to Is-sa-ki-ep. After another brief consultation, Beaver told Marcy, "He say, sir, you the strangest man he never see; every man he seen before, when he been travelin' long time, the fust thing he want, *wife.*"

Leaving the emigrant train at Santa Fe, the colonel explored south along the Rio Grande to Dona Ana and returned northeastward, across the Pecos and lower Llano Estacado, to Indian Territory and Arkansas. He was deeply interested in Beaver, and while they were bivouacked alone one night, asked the Indian if he was married.

After a long pause, the Delaware gave his forefinger a twirl to imitate the throwing of a lasso, and replied: "One time me catch 'um wife. I pay one hoss — one saddle — one bridle — two plug tobacco, and plenty goods. I take him to my house — got plenty meat — plenty corn — plenty everything. One time me take a walk, maybe so two-three hours. When I come home, the womans say, 'Black Beaver, what for you go way long time?' I say, 'I not go nowhere; I just take littel walk.' Then that womans get heap mad, and say, 'No, Black Beaver, you not take no littel walk. I know what for you go way — *see nodder one womans.*' I say, 'Maybe not.' Then that womans he cry long time, and all e'time now he mad. You never see 'Merican womans that way?"

Marcy agreed that white women were not peculiar in that respect.

"What you do for cure him?" Beaver asked. "Whip him?"

Marcy explained that these chronic and vexatious complaints could not be benefited by such treatment, even when administered in homoeo-

13

pathic doses, and added: "I believe it is now admitted by all sensible men that it is better to let nature take its course and trust to merciful Providence."

Beaver looked dejected. Finally he brightened again, and remarked triumphantly: "I tell you, my friend, what I do; when I go home, I ketch 'um nodder wife."

He remained with Marcy, however, until the colonel had established Fort Arbuckle near Wild Horse Creek, west of the Washita. Most Chickasaws had moved out into their "district" and shooting soldiers were needed where the Plains tribes were pestering their newer settlements. After that Beaver assisted the army in exploring the country lying upon the headwaters of the Canadian, Trinity, Brazos and Colorado rivers of Texas, heretofore a *terra incognita*.

In 1852, when Major George Anderson and his troops of the 7th Infantry assumed command at Arbuckle, and Marcy went to Fort Washita to prepare for his expedition up the Arkansas, Beaver decided to quit roaming the West. He took a permanent wife and chose a tract of land near Arbuckle, where other Delawares were then living.

When Lieutenant A.W. Whipple visited the fort in 1853, hoping to employ him for an exploring party seeking a railroad route westward from Fort Smith, he found Beaver in his cabin, sitting cross-legged, smoking his pipe, in perfect tranquility. "He was a meager-looking man of middle size," Whipple reported. "His long black hair framed a face that was clever, but which bore a melancholy expression of sickness and sorrow, though more than forty winters could not have passed over it."

Beaver refused the lieutenant's proposal, although it was more money than he had ever been offered. Three days of pleading were in vain. "I have accompanied 'Mericans in great war — I have brought home more scalps from hunting trips than you can lift —I have seen Pacific Ocean seven times and should like to see salt water once more; but I am ill and might die and be buried away from my people," Beaver said.

Whipple finally discovered the real reason. His wife opposed his leaving her and their young son for so long a time. All the lieutenant received was advice from the canny guide.

It was different when Lieutenant Arthur D. Free of the 2nd Dragoons, with a detachment of twenty men, arrived at Arbuckle March 13, 1854, on a hunt for Indians who had murdered Colonel Jesse Stern, Indian agent, on the Brazos. Black Beaver was sent for and soon learned from some Kickapoos that a member of their tribe, Sa-Kok-wah, and a half-breed had committed the crime. The pair were captured and slain by their own people.

Explorers and travelers continued to seek Beaver's assistance. He didn't mine interpreting and giving advice, but long journeys were taboo. Besides a wife and son, he had two daughters. He had learned to farm and was developing a fine herd of cattle. He enlarged his log house, adding a front porch and two fireplaces. The Delawares now regarded him as their leader, and upon him fell the honor of keeping the Great Treaty parchment given them by William Penn and handed down for generations from one leader to another.

The forts across Indian Territory grew, their detachments ranged far and wide, and the wild Plains tribes became less and less hostile. The "Leased District" had been obtained for them from the Chickasaws, and Beaver, like many other settlers, looked forward to a period of peace and prosperity.

Then, far away in the East, came rumbles of the Civil War. As Indian Territory became more

15

and more a powder keg, Beaver grew concerned. Late in April, 1861, he went to consult with Colonel William H. Emory, a cavalry officer he had known during the Mexican War and now in command of all troops in the Territory with headquarters at Fort Washita. There he learned that the South had seceded from the Union, and as the Chickasaw and Choctaw were slave owners, the garrison was completely surrounded by Southern sympathizers.

Emory had orders to concentrate all forces at Forts Cobb, Washita and Arbuckle at Fort Arbuckle and withdraw them en masse, but already 4,000 Rebels from Texas were marching on the garrison and 2,000 were moving to stike his flank from Arkansas. The only chance for his comparatively small command was to take to the open prairies northwest. Guides were essential, but none of the Indians "upon whom the government had lavished its bounty" would aid him.

Beaver volunteered. "I need not say how invaluable was his service and great his sacrifice," Emory wrote. "He was the first to give me the information by which I was enabled to capture the enemy's advance guard, the first prisoners captured in the war."

Without the loss of a man, horse or wagon, Black Beaver led his 750 soldiers and 150 non-combatants across the Cherokee Outlet and the site of present Wichita, Kansas, to the safety of Fort Leavenworth. So hasty had been the departure there had been no time to return to his family, his farm well stocked with horses and cattle, his fields of corn. He had even left behind his most precious possession — the Penn parchment.

Beaver started back to the Washita. En route he met bands of Wichitas and Delawares and his own family fleeing the Confederate invasion. The Chickasaws, Choctaws and Texans, they told him, were burning buildings and confiscating property of Indians loyal to the Union. His home had been reduced to ashes, including the Great Treaty parchment.

Beaver turned back with his people to Kansas, where he and 170 Delaware warriors joined a militia company for the duration. Although Emory and several of his officers testified to the old Delaware's patriotism, the only compensation he received from the Federal government was a small per cent of his actual loss.

He was still in Kansas in 1866 when the Delaware tribe was informed that by remaining in the Sunflower State they would automatically become United States citizens, which would cost them their headrights. Beaver suggested an alternative — move into the Cherokee Nation. At the close of the war, the Union, considering the Cherokees sympathetic to the South, had imposed upon them the provision that they must admit "friendly and civilized tribes" into their boundaries. The Delawares quickly began negotiations.

A delegation representing both tribes went to Washington. Black Beaver accompanied the chiefs as spokesman. An agreement was reached whereby 985 registered Delawares became Cherokee citizens with equal rights and land totaling 157,600 acres.

Many other members of the tribe, under the informal title of "absentee" Delawares, chose to return to the Washita where they had lived before the war. They were moved to the Wichita-Caddo reserve, near Anadarko. Beaver and his family went with them.

At age 61, Beaver made a new start. Agent William B. Hazen, writing the Indian Bureau in 1869, stated that he has a large farm under cultivation, lives in a very comfortable manner, and has good, substantial frontier buildings. He is respected by all Indians who know him, and his influence with them is always good. He is a Christian (having joined the Baptist Mission church), and tries to do what is right in the sight of God and toward his fellowmen . . . .

Beaver did all he could to encourage belligerent tribes to accept reservation life. He interpreted for every agent and missionary in the Territory, made oral translations of the Bible, and was in demand as a speechmaker.

He had no time for regrets and resentments and did not believe in pacification. As a delegate to the International Indian Council at Okmulgee in 1870, where an inquiry was made into the conduct of the Kiowas and Comanches who had been raiding into Texas, Beaver criticized the speeches of the delegates from the Five Civilized Tribes as being too mild and proposed to talk "plainly and brutally" to the wild Indians.

At the International Council at Anadarko in August of 1872, he pleaded with all tribes present to

make one road and travel it. My red brethren just like wild ones (here pointing to the Kiowas and Comanches). They say to United States, "Here my war hatchet; no more war," then break treaty. At that time Indians had mighty good chiefs (meaning Satank and Satanta); they dead now, but young chiefs all here to carry out same provisions — "Keep war hatchet buried . . . ." We all want peace among our-

selves and with United States. We
want our country; we love it all here together. Well now after we make friends,
all of us, no more bad, then we are no
more afraid to go anywhere; go all over
United States; meet white man; he ask
what tribe you from; we tell him; he
say that is mighty good Indian. We like
that. I hope we all united together, all
chiefs that's what we want — peace.
That much I talk to my brothers.

He asked all Indians to help in getting the
Kiowas and Comanches out of trouble and per-
suade them to make terms with the government,
and told them that

a good many times I hungry. When I
come home, I'm not satisfied. I travel
all over western country, I have pretty
hard troubles, sometimes have eat
mule for month. I did not want to, but
have to, to save my life. Then I travel
south, settle down, make farm and
raise corn. Now I never hungry. I know
how to raise corn. I very sorry I didn't
began raise corn when young man.

In January 1873, Black Beaver visited his Quaker agent friend, Lawrie Tatum, at the Kiowa-
Comanche Agency. He made a personal appeal
to the Indians to

stop raiding . . . send children to
school, settle down, do as Quakers wish
you do. Quakers your friends; they
made treaty with Delawares near 200
years ago, which both parties bound
themselves and children after them, to
be friends to each other, forever. This
treaty never been broken.

It was the Cheyennes, smarting under the change in their way of life and the extermination of the buffalo by hunters on the Texas plains, who finally broke off their reservation and launched the Indian War of 1874. Beaver was "greatly saddened," but felt some consolation in that only part of the Kiowas and Comanches and none of the other tribes had joined them.

The war was disastrous, as Beaver had predicted. In 1878, thirty-four tribes were represented at the Grand Council which met at Okmulgee in an effort to form an Indian state with representatives and a governor — a matter they had discussed for eight years. Black Beaver was in great demand as interpreter.

On June 2, Agent P.B. Hunt, at Anadarko, wrote the Commissioner of Indian Affairs in Washington:

> On the 8th day of May, Black Beaver, the most prominent of all Indians belonging to the old Wichita Agency, died suddenly of heart disease . . . . His burial took place the day following his death, and more than 150 persons showed the esteem in which he was held by following his remains to their last earthly resting place. The coffin was borne by Agency employes and other white residents, and the burial services were conducted by the Delawares led by their Seminole preacher.

Black Beaver was a man of stature. Even tribesmen who refused to follow his example of untiring industry and desire to be a useful citizen respected him. He was exceedingly proud of his skin color, but he was first an American.

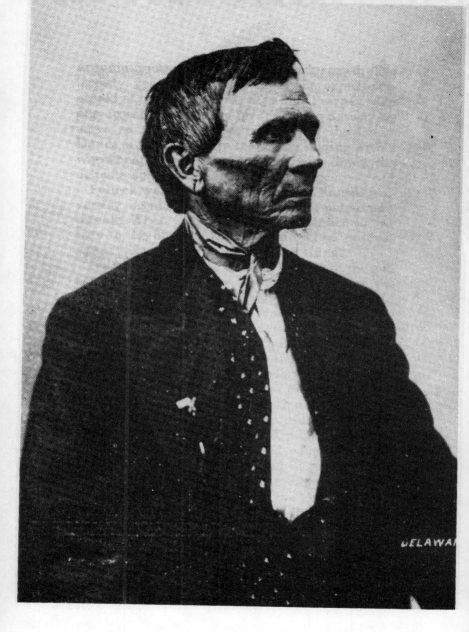

BLACK BEAVER (side view showing resemblance to Abraham Lincoln).

WILLIAM PENN signing treaty with Delaware Indians at Shackamaxon (from painting by Benjamin West). To Black Beaver fell the honor of keeping the original parchment, handed down from leader to leader for almost 200 years.

DELAWARE-CHEROKEE delegation in Washington, 1866. (L to R, standing: James Daniel, Black Beaver, Henry Tiblow, John Pratt, Charles Armstrong and John Young. L to R, seated: James Ketcham, James Connor, John Connor, Charles Journeycake, Isaac Journeycake and Capt. John Sarcoxie.)

23

COLONEL RANDOLPH B. MARCY, the noted pathfinder, who employed Black Beaver on several occasions and praised him as an intelligent Indian who proved to be most useful.

2. Bard of the Oktahutchee

Every Western history buff knows the story of Sequoyah who, solely from the resources of his own mind and without knowledge of any language other than Cherokee, conceived and perfected an entire alphabet or syllabary that made his tribe one of the most literate of the Indian Nations. And every student of history knows that he accomplished in twelve years that which took Egyptian, Phoenician and Greek scholars more than 3,000 years to develop. By the 1830s, when his people were removed into Oklahoma over the Trail of Tears, ninety percent of them could read and write.

Not so well known, however, is the story of his proponent of communication, Alexander Lawrence Posey — Creek poet, humorist, philosopher, and the most famous Indian dialect writer produced by the confederacy known as the Five Civilized Tribes.

Posey was a man of striking appearance, who usually dressed in tailored attire, with white hat, immaculate gloves and a stick. As one prominent territorial journalist described him, "his complexion was swarthy, his long hair glossy black, and his eyes brilliant, dark and expressive. His features bore marked resemblance to those of Shelley. His imagination, tinged with the melancholy of his race, and his love of nature, tender and romantic, were inheritances from tribal generations that knew all the ways of the wind, the sky and the earth."

Indeed it is doubtful if any other man in America showed more genius in human understanding and unusual comprehension of the red man's soul and spirit during the transition period in which a genuine, deep Indian culture was being welded, sometimes in grief and torture, with that of the white man. He was as steadfast in his belief as Sequoyah that the progress of civilization paralleled the evolution of the written word.

Posey was born August 3, 1873, near Limbo creek, in present McIntosh County. His father, Lewis H. "Hence" Posey, was a fine specimen of the Irish race and a son of white intruders who had wandered into the Creek country from Texas about 1841. Hence Posey's parents had died when he was a baby and he had been reared by a Creek woman near Fort Gibson in the Cherokee Nation, where he attended a school taught by the noted missionary Lewis Robertson and gained a knowledge of the English language and mathematics. A jovial, mirth-loving man, he never lost an opportunity for a practical joke, and this trait was prevalent in his son Alex. For a time Hence Posey had served as a United States deputy marshal at Fort Smith, Arkansas. In October, 1872, he had married a girl of a fine Creek Indian family, and established himself on a large farm up the North Canadian River eight miles west of Eufaula, at Bald Hill, Alex's birthplace.

Alex's mother was the daughter of Pohas Harjo, a Creek full blood. Her English name was Nancy Phillips. She belonged to the Wind Clan, the strongest clan of the Creeks, and was a member of the Tuskegee Town or Band of the Muskogee nation. Though uneducated and unable to speak English, she possessed a rare native sense. She was a tidy housekeeper and careful in her personal appearance, with the Indian fondness for decided colors. A sincere and devout Christian, she offered her prayers with earnestness and eloquence, in her own tongue. She gave full time to the comfort of her family and saw to it that there was always an abundance of wholesome food on the table. If little was left from the midday meal, she baked an extra pan of bread so that they might have all they wished to eat for supper. In hot weather, she frequently doused her head and the heads of the children with cold water as a protection from extreme heat.

The old law of the rod was in vogue in the Posey household. Alex recalled that he

> was raised on a farm and accounted a pretty weedy crop. The cockleburs and crabgrass grew all the more prolifically after I had been given a good thrashing. I grew into manhood with Tom, a fullblood Creek orphan, whom father had adopted. Tom's sense of humor and my love for pranks got us into much trouble.

Once when Mrs. Posey put them to some task at the homestead, they went about it with such "characteristic deliberation" that she remarked they moved as though they had stones on their backs. It was a suggestion. When she reappeared a few minutes later, she found the boys in the barn-lot with rocks tied to their backs, carrying them about.

Again, when she put the boys to work in the garden, promising to return shortly to check their progress, they spent the interlude digging a hole in the garden path and neatly camouflaging it with small sticks and earth. When Mrs. Posey returned, she fell into the hole. A stout paling fence prevented the lads from escaping; they were caught and soundly whipped.

Alex accepted punishment as a matter of course. It was always administered in the spirit of wholesome correction; he was never humiliated, nor the natural inclination of his mind repressed. Stubbornness and resentment were not in him. He was a child of deep feeling, of quick, accurate observation, often self-conscious and reflective, and loved the streams and hills, prairies, trees, flowers, birds, animals, the tangled wildwood, the heavens at night and the magnificent cloud displays at sunset.

For summer wear, Mrs. Posey made the boys single flowing garments which reached the heels. Memory of these remained with the poet in after years, for he said of them:

> I often look back to the "days of lost sunshine", when Tom and I romped in our long shirts, or "sweeps," as we called them. There was a vast freedom in these gowns; freedom for the wind to play in, and they were so easily thrown aside at the "old swimming hole." We looked forward with regret to the time when we would have to discard them for jean-coats and trousers and copper-toed boots, though these were desirable to chase rabbits on a snowy day. Those who have never worn "sweeps" have never known half the secrets whispered by the winds of boyhood.

Alex's education began when he was seven. A private tutor was his first experience. In one of his writings, Alex described him as "a dried-up, hard-up, weazen-faced, irritable little fellow, with an appetite that caused the better dishes on our table to disappear rapidly." His father had picked him up somewhere, and noting his "bookish turn," given him a place in the family. He taught Alex the alphabet and to read short sentences.

Although Alex understood English fairly well, its construction was so different from his native tongue that he feared to trust himself in the use of it. He never spoke English until compelled to by his father:

One evening when I blurted out in the best Creek I could command, and began telling him about a horse-hunt, he cut me off shortly: "Look here, young man, if you don't tell me that in English after supper I am going to wear you out." I was hungry, but this put an abrupt end to my desire for the good things heaped on my plate.

I got up from the table and made myself useful — brought water from the well, turned the cows into the pasture — thinking this would cause him to forget what he had said. My goodness, however, was without avail, for as soon as he came from the table he asked me in a gentle but firm voice to relate the horse-hunt. Well, he was so pleased with my English that he never afterwards allowed me to speak Creek.

When Alex had completed the Creek Second Reader, he was sent to the public (Indian) school at Eufaula. He showed a strong knack for learning. During the long winter evenings, sitting about the blazing fagots in the open fireplace, he listened to the legends, mythology and folklore of his race as related by his mother. His sensitive mind absorbed these tales of simple, happy life of the Creeks in their primitive forest before the white man came, of their proud tribal history when they were still free men and lords of the earth, peopled with characters as fascinating and fantastic as any created by Shakespeare. They stirred the soul of this Creek boy and became the inspiration of his already delicate perception of the charms of nature.

His desire to write did not develop until he entered Bacone Indian University at Muskogee, at age seventeen. Alex was timid and reserved, but under the kind and thoughtful guidance of President A.C. Bacone, he soon plunged into campus activities with enthusiasm. He worked as school librarian on Sundays. After school hours on week days he set type for the school paper called the *Instructor*.

Meanwhile, his father moved to Eufaula, where he operated a hotel to help the family income, the farm at Bald Hill proving inadequate. George Riley Hall, who was teaching in the Creek national schools, stopped at the hotel one evening for lodging. Mr. Posey explained that the hotel was full, but he might stay if he would share his son's room in the attic. Alex was home from Bacone at the time. Mr. Posey called the boy over and introduced him. Hall remembered that

> he was 18 — a shy, slim youth. In his attic room I found he had a number of volumes neatly arranged on a home-made bookshelf. The old masters in English and American literature crowded each other. He asked if I liked to read and if I liked poetry. That was the beginning. I did like poetry and I found myself liking the Indian boy. We read and chatted until the early hours of the morning. From that time we were boon companions . . . .
>
> Alex could read beautifully. His voice was low-pitched, his enunciation faultless. His soul was attuned to the sublime. He loved sonorous sounds and musical cadences. If his sophomoric tendencies smacked of the bombastic at that time, it was distinctly to his credit rather than otherwise. His taste was surprisingly correct, even in his school days.

In October 1892, he made his first contribution to the literary world. His poem, "The Comet's Tale," depicting the Indian version of the coming of the first ships of the white men to America, appeared in the *Instructor*. His next effort was an article entitled "The Indian: 'What of Him?'" This was followed by "The Sea God," "Death of A Window Plant," "The River Strange," and "Fixico Yahola's Revenge," the story of an ancient warrior who assumed the form of a bear.

His writings appeared over his nom de plume *Chinnubbie Harjo*. Chinnubbie Harjo, in Creek mythology, originally had been a mighty man endowed with supernatural powers, but so burdened with the many foibles and weaknesses of humanity that he had changed character and was regarded as an evil genius. He was to the ancient Creeks what Hiawatha was to the Iroquois — what Manabozho was to the Algonquins. Alex Posey chose to portray him in his modified capacity, and published four separate works on him in pamphlet form entitled "Chinnubbie Harjo, the Evil Genius of the Creeks," "Chinnubbie's Courtship," "Chinnubbie and the Owl," and "Chinnubbie Scalps the Squaws."

Alex graduated from Bacone in the spring of 1895, and attracted wide attention with his commencement address on "Does It Pay to Educate the Indian?" His genuine interest in the subject and the fervor of his delivery made it one of the outstanding addresses ever given at an Indian institute by a student.

After graduation, Alex returned to Bald Hill. The Creek national government was undergoing some revolutionary changes in which his father played a major part. Isparchecher, the Union Indian who had joined old Chief Apothleyahola and Penwa Harjo in their trek to Kansas during the Civil War, was a candidate for principal

31

chief. Hence Posey not only espoused Isparchecher's cause, but was largely responsible for en-
gineering his campaign to a successful conclu-
sion. Irregularities were discovered on the books
of the Creek national treasurer. This official was
suspended by executive order and Alex Posey appointed to replace him.

A beardless youngster with such responsibility caused considerable apprehension. But Alex
acquitted himself admirably. Okmulgee, then a
struggling village, was the capital of the nation.
The old rock-walled Council House was one of
the most interesting, picturesque places in Indian Territory. There were rooms where the different departments of Creek government was administered and halls where the two branches of
their remnant of sovereignty, the House of Warriors and the House of Kings, held sessions. Here
Alex came to know the statesmen of those early
years, the chieftains, educators, stern-faced jus-
tices, Indian police, and the hopes and problems
of his people under pressure to accept citizenship
in the future state.

Politics and political conspiracies, however,
did not appeal to the literary nature of young
Posey. When his term ended, he prevailed on his
father to secure him a position in educational
work. In 1896, he became superintendent of the
Creek orphans school at Okmulgee. In May of
that year he married Miss Minnie Harris, of Fay-
etteville, Arkansas.

Alex said of their romance:

> I was introduced to her one morning
> by J.B. Thornton, "ye" editor of the *In-
> dian Journal,* at breakfast in a hotel at
> Eufaula. The beauty of the young
> school teacher thoroughly charmed me,
> and though I saw her frequently, I
> could not sufficiently overcome my In-

dian nature to talk with her. She went away. I thought of her constantly; would sometimes grow anxious to declare my love by letter. Two months passed, and she returned to take up her work. One day I made it convenient to pass the school-house. I got a glimpse of her as I hurried by on "Ballie" (his horse) and another as I returned. My love grew deeper. One night I was in Eufaula, and by chance met her. I offered her a place (as matron) in my school; she accepted, and when summer was come again, "two hearts beat as one."

Minnie proved an ideal companion. She saved him much "bother and vexation" in looking after details at the orphanage. He devoted much time to a close reading of Plutarch's Lives, and familiarized himself with ancient history. In October 1897, he resigned to settle on a farm he purchased on the North Canadian, near Stidham.

Two months later, however, he was called to the superintendency of the Creek National High School at Eufaula. After putting the administration of its affairs on a satisfactory basis, he was asked to do the same for a similar institution at Wetumka.

Meanwhile, he wrote as inspiration prompted him. His wife managed the farm and his business affairs. There were tenants to be reckoned with, but she never allowed him to be disturbed. He wrote during the morning, and in the afternoon would walk in the fields. The whole world was in tune for him. In this atmosphere of contentment and tranquility, he dreamed of a future devoted entirely to literature, and produced many of his sweetest poems.

His communion with the flowers and birds inspired "To A Daffodil"—

Out in the golden air,
　Out where the skies are fair,
I hear a song of gladness,
　With never note of sadness,
Sing out thy heart's delight,
　And mine of every sorrow.
Sing, sweet bird, till the night,
　And come again tomorrow.

and "To An Indian Meadow Lark"—

When other birds despairing south-
ward fly,
　In early autumn-time away;
When all the green leaves of the forest
die,
　How merry still art thou, and gay.

O! golden-breasted bird of dawn,
　Through all the bleak days singing
on,
Till winter, wooed a captive by thy
strain,
　Breaks into smiles, and spring is
come again.

On viewing the skull and bones of a wolf, he
wrote:

How savage, fierce and grim!
　His bones are bleached and white.
But what is death to him?
　He grins as if to bite . . . .

In the Tulledega Hills along the river east of
his home, Alex and George Riley Hall wandered
many times. "We did not talk much — just loit-

ered," Hall said. "The place was wild and indescribably beautiful. Rapids in the river at one point amounted almost to a waterfall. The roar of this water reverberated musically when the air was right for echoes." It was here Posey got his inspiration for the three verses of "In Tulledega"—

Where mountains lift their heads
   To clouds that nestle low;
Where constant beauty spreads
   Sublimer scenes below;

Where gray and massive rocks
   O'erhang rough heights sublime;
Where awful grandeur mocks
   The brush, and poet's rhyme,

We saw the evening blush
   Above the rugged range,
We heard the river rush
   Far off and faint and strange.

Hall considered these lines "exquisite — a cut gem, unexcelled in American literature." Such was the dreamy side of this versatile man. He responded instantly to such influences. No wonder there was little conversation. They needed little.

Alex loved the beautiful North Canadian, named by the Creeks, "Oktahutchee" (sandy river). He made canoe trips down it often and recorded his impressions in "Song of the Oktahutchee" —

Far, far, far are my silver waters
drawn;
   The hills embrace me, loth to let me
go;

The maidens think me fair to look
upon,
    And trees lean over, glad to hear me
flow.
Thro' field and valley, green because of
me,
    I wander, wander to the distant
sea . . . .

Though he had no premonition of the fate that
would befall him nearly a decade later, there
came from his pen "My Fancy" —

Why do trees along the river
    Lean so far out o'er the tide?
Very wise men tell me why, but
    I am never satisfied;
And so I keep my fancy still,
    That trees lean out to save
The drowning from the clutches of
    The cold, remorseless wave.

From October, 1897 to 1899 was unquestionab-
ly the golden era of Alex Posey's life. He was a
loving husband and indulgent father. His son,
Irving Yahola, and a daughter were born at Stidham. His great love for his mother was an added
inspiration, and he never failed to be with her at
Christmas time.

In 1899, he resigned from the Wetumka school
to take charge of the Eufaula *Indian Journal,*
where he had his greatest literary opportunity.
The Dawes Commission was closing its work
with the Five Civilized Tribes. Sentiment among
members of the Creek Nation was sharply divided. Posey sought to express his opinion and the
opinions of tribal leaders in a series of letters
dealing with the graft and plunder that was
rapidly displacing the Indian in his native land.
Written in a dialect used by the red man who

could not accustom himself to the idioms of the English language, they purported to be conversations between Wolf Warrior, Hot Gun and Tookpofko Micco, old Creek men, and white men prominent in Indian Territory affairs.

The latter he spoke of with the following names: Tams Bixby, Commissioner to the Five Tribes, was "Toms Big Pie"; Pliny Soper was "Plinty-so-far"; Secretary of the Interior E.A. Hitchcock was "Secretary Its-Cocked"; Charles N. Haskell, who became Oklahoma's first governor, was "C.N. Has-it"; and Senator Robert L. Owen was "Colonel Robert L. Owes-em."

These inimitable writings, known as the "Fus Fixico Letters," made an immediate hit. They were reprinted as soon as published by almost every major newspaper in the Territory, and many outside it. His comments on the statehood question attracted interest as far away as London, and won him the reputation of being the first Indian humorist and satirist.

It is doubtful Posey accomplished his purpose. But he kept the *Indian Journal* in the very front rank of territorial newspapers and developed an entirely new field in literature. Until that time it had been believed that the Indian, grim and stoical, was incapable of facetious allusions to himself and others.

His editorial columns took on added brilliance as he lampooned democrats and republicans alike. Federal affairs were handled at Muskogee by republicans. The democrats grew restless and sought to unhorse some of the carpetbaggers by empaneling a grand jury. They appealed to United States District Attorney William Melette. Melette's evasion of a direct refusal by saying the weather was too hot brought from Posey this biting irony:

It's too hot yet
Says Bill Melette;
He'll wait till frost, no doubt,
It's too hot yet
For Bill Melette
To turn the rascals out.

Posey's popularity brought him many offers from people and institutions of this Indian country metropolis. In March 1902, he bought half-interest in the Muskogee *Times*. This venture lasted only a few months, however.

In the readjustment incident to allotment in severalty to the Indians by the Dawes Commission, much land remained unappraised and many "lost Creeks" — those who had married into other tribes or wandered away to live in seclusion — had to be located and enrolled. If any Indian failed to take his allotment, the land would be disposed of with little consideration for his interest. And there were Creek babies born after the original rolls had closed that had to be sought out and listed. It was work that only a man familiar with every phase of Indian life and character could accomplish. Because of his understanding for the ignorant people of his tribe, Alex gave up newspapering to take charge of the Creek Enrollment Field Party of the Commission to the Five Civilized Tribes.

The Indians trusted Posey. For three years he traveled by wagon and horseback into every nook and corner of the nation, accompanied only by Drennon C. Skaggs, a notary public and stenographer. Scores of affidavits were secured from witnesses in citizenship cases pending before the Commission who could not go to Muskogee at their own expense to testify, and hundreds of "lost" Indians and babies were enrolled on the roadsides, in the tangled forests, at the hearthside, and in the cotton patch.

Posey's greatest problem was to search out and conciliate the "Snakes" — a Creek faction led by Chief Crazy Snake (Chitto Harjo), who refused to have their lands divided and surrender their tribal authority.

Crazy Snake exerted great influence in his tribe. The Indians listened to his moving eloquence before the assembled Kings and Warriors of the legislature and his patriotic plea to hold the land "so long as grass shall grow or water run." When the Curtis Act of 1898 put the finishing touches to the work of the Dawes Commission, abolishing tribal laws and courts, he called his followers together at Hickory Ground, which he proclaimed the new capital of the nation. Laws were passed forbidding Creeks to employ white men or rent land to them. Indian police were appointed to enforce these decrees. The farmers in the area became uneasy and sought refuge at Henryetta. The situation was aggravated by a lynching at Henryetta by this rebellious government-within-a-government.

Alex was diplomatic. His experience in government work had sharpened his natural ability. He inveigled Crazy Snake into signing a certain paper which proved afterwards to be an acceptance of his allotment.

When Crazy Snake learned of what he regarded "the perfidy of his young friend," his fury was boundless. Alex managed to avoid him for a time, but eventually had to face the old patriot.

Posey, in Creek, means "cat." Little cat, or kitten, becomes "Posochee," with the accent on the first syllable. As Alex described their meeting, the old man stood erect with folded arms, contenting himself several minutes by burning down the young poet with his commanding, challenging, piercing black eyes. Alex could feel himself shrinking under his withering gaze. Finally, the old chief delivered this devastating broadside in

39

biting, scornful tones, unhurried and deliberate:

> Posochee! Posochee! You of the forked tongue! Traitor! Liar! Posochee! Posochee! You came to me with the sweet words of your Indian mother. I listened, and believed you. Posochee! Posochee! Your weasel words came to me in the soft tones of the Indian and won my trust. You betrayed me. You deceived me. The forked tongue of your white father led you to shame. You shame me and you shame yourself. Posochee. My eyes are tired of seeing you. Begone!

Alex lost no time taking the old chief at his word.

He was an ardent admirer of Crazy Snake and considered him the last true son of a fading race. A posse attacked the camp at Henryetta. After a three-hour battle, the insurgents surrendered. Crazy Snake's detention in the federal jail at Muskogee by the United States authorities moved Posey to pen these lines of tribute:

> Down with him! chain him! bind him fast!
> Slam the iron door and turn the key!
> The one true Creek, perhaps the last
> To dare declare, "You have wronged me!"
> Defiant, stoical, silent,
> Suffers imprisonment!
>
> Such coarse black hair! such eagle eye!
> Such stately mien! — how arrow-straight!
> Such will! such courage to defy
> The powerful makers of his fate!

A traitor, outlaw — what you will,
He is the noble red man still.

Condemn him and his kind to shame!
I bow to him, exalt his name!

The people of Indian Territory realized that statehood was inevitable. The wiser men of the tribes thought it best to take concerted action and thereby secure equal influence in public affairs. Accordingly, in August 1905, they met at Muskogee and formulated a constitution for a separate commonwealth. Posey was one of the delegates and was elected convention secretary. The simple, terse English of the constitution was principally his work. And it was he who proposed "Sequoyah" as the name for the Indian state, in tribute to the famous Cherokee.

The document, duly submitted to Congress, received no favorable action and was never revived. Notwithstanding the fact that it appeared impractical to those who had been through the struggle over single and double statehood in the western half of Oklahoma, the Sequoyah movement proved very beneficial in preparing the Indian mind for the change when it did come, as evidenced in Posey's last Fus Fixico letter on June 27, 1907:

Hotgun take his sofky jar to a shady place an' call in his old friends for a discussion . . . .

"Well so," Hotgun he say, "I like to know who done it, anyhow."

An' Tookpofko Micco he smoke 'is ol' hatchet-pipe slow an' say, "Well, so, in olden times, seven cities want to be Homer's birthplace; an' same way, all the politicians claim the credit for statehood an' dispute with one 'nother.

Delegate Makefire (Congressman Bird S. McGuire) he say he done it an' couldn't tell a lie. He say if fight he put up for statehood wasn't worth a decent burial in the Statesman's Corner o' the capital buildin' it wasn't worth takin' the Father o' His Country's example in vain. Clarence Rug-last (Cononel Clarence B. Douglas, prominent Muskogee newspaperman) say he done it — with Washington *Post* interviews written by 'imself — an' he want a outside lot facin' the main aisle in the Poet's Corner; also 'is statue, with a sword buckled on, standin' 'straddle o' lot o' carpetbaggers. An' they was some commission court lawyers an' not'ry publics claim the honor, too, but they wasn't entitled to it no more'n Crazy Snake."

Then Hotgun he say, "Well, so Delegate Makefire an' Clarence Rug-last was imposin' on that razorback the statehood rooters take to Congress las' winter an' someone ought to report 'em to the humane society."

Wolf Warrior he give big grunt an' spit in the ragweeds an' pay close 'tention.

Then Hotgun he go on an' say, "Well so before statehood they was too much sentiment mixed up in the Injin problem. The missionary he tell the Injin he must lay up treasures in heaven, but didn't show 'im how to keep body an' soul together on earth an' lay by for the rainy day; an' the school teacher he learn 'im how to read an' shade 'is letters when he write, but didn't teach 'im how to make two blades o' grass grow

42

out o' one; an' the philanthropist re-
mind 'im o' the century o' dishonor, instead o' the future individual responsibility; an' the government dish out beef
an' annuity to 'im instead of a mule an'
a plow. Everything like that make Injin no count, except give jobs to government clerks."

An' Tookpofko Micco he say, "Well,
so the ol' order was passed away.
Maybe so now the politician tell the
Injin how to win salvation in the democrat party, or republican party, an'
party bosses teach 'im how to put in
two votes instead o' one."

Then Hotgun he go on an' say, "Well,
so if the Injin know 'is business, he
was better off than before. All he had
to do was be a Injin an' stay to 'imself
like an ol' bull in winter time. He don't
want to be democrat or republican.
Maybe so 'im hair was long enough for
a populist, but he better not. If he take
sides he won't 'mount to nothin' an'
couldn't be dog pelter."

An' Tookpofko Micco he say, "Well,
so I was raised on democrat sofky an'
don't care who find it out, but I don't
vote for yellow dogs on 'count o' the
color."

Wolf Warrior grunt an' spit in ragweeds ag'in an' move further in shade.

Then Hotgun he go on an' say, "Well,
so we was all one people now an' neighbors, anyhow, regardless o' race or politics or religion. Instead o' Choctaws
an' Chickasaws an' Seminoles an'
Creeks an' Cherokees an' Boomer an'
Osages an' Sequoyahans, we was all
Oklahomans. Muskogee wasn't in Injin

Territory an' Oklahoma City wasn't in Short Grass country. You didn't have to slip over the line for the stomach's sake now. You c'n be at home in Beaver county same as at Hickory Ground. You could say, 'I'm from Oklahoma,' an' be proud of it same as if you was from Ol' Dominion."

Posey's work with the Dawes Commission had ended. So had his era of communal living. But he was confident that he could adjust to the new order of things. He still had his home on the North Canadian. There, too, was his birthplace and the graves of his ancestors.

He decided to return to the *Indian Journal*. His knowledge of the country and its people would enable him also to deal successfully in lands, timber and minerals. On May 27, 1908, he closed his affairs at Muskogee and with R.D. Howe, an attorney, boarded the train for Eufaula.

Heavy rains the day before had swollen the Canadian beyond its banks. The train stopped at the river. The road bed and track had been washed out, making it impossible to go on.

Posey and Howe talked it over. As their business in Eufaula was urgent, they arranged for a Negro to row them across the river, intending to continue the journey on foot.

In mid-stream the Negro lost his paddle and the boat became unmanageable. The current, rushing toward the break in the fill, sucked the boat against the right-of-way fence, where it capsized. The Negro drowned immediately. Howe swam to safety.

Posey caught the branch of a small willow. For more than two hours he clung there, while crowds came from Eufaula with another boat and a rope to rescue him.

But Posey's strength was exhausted. At the

CHITTO HARJO (Crazy Snake), leader of a mutinous faction of the Creeks, whom Posey sought to conciliate while in charge of the Creek Enrollment Field Party.

ISPARHECHER, Principal Chief of the Creek Nation, who appointed the 22-year-old Posey as national treasurer.

A GROUP OF THE "Snake Band" of Creek Indian insurgents under arrest at Muskogee following their surrender at Henryetta.

CREEK NATIONAL HIGH SCHOOL at Eufaula, where Posey served as
superintendent in 1897.

ALEXANDER LAWRENCE POSEY (as editor of the Eufaula Indian Journal, ca. 1899).

point of being saved, he lost his grasp on the rope that had been thrown him and he was swept away in the raging torrent — the beloved Oktahutchee of his dreams and poems.

3. Rough Rider of the Pawnees

Although William Pollock never reached the pinnacle of success in his world of art, he ranked among the top Indian artists of America. His childhood playmates remembered him as a quiet lad, with little to say and shunning all tribal games and athletics. To his fellow tribesmen, he remained an enigmatic individual constantly searching for new horizons. He appeared to be wasting his time sketching birds and animals in the sand with a sharp stick. The boy was "mixed up," they said. According to his half brother, Eagle Chief, "He never seemed to know what he really wanted."

That William Pollock achieved fame is a matter of record. What is not generally understood is the internal turmoil that tormented the sinewy, 5-foot-8 Indian while he sought an express purpose for his life.

The quest began the day he was born on the Pawnee reservation in Nebraska in 1872. He was a full blood whose Indian name was *Syracrisout-Kuwyh*. At age three, he came with his tribe to Oklahoma. As the Indians grew accustomed to the white man's ways, they gave white names to their children. While attending the reservation school at the Pawnee Agency, *Syracrisout-Kuwyh* became William Pollock, namesake of an inspector in the Indian service and later agent for the Osages at Pawhuska. From the agency school, young Pollock advanced to the Haskell Institute at Lawrence, Kansas, in 1884.

At Haskell Institute, William sought desperately to find himself. Uncommunicative and apparently morose, it was difficult to ascertain to what extent he comprehended his instructor. One classmate recalled that he "tried everything from the shoe shop and bakery to carpentry and the paint shop."

In the paint shop he showed a natural talent for blending colors, and suddenly remembered the birds and animals he used to sketch in the sand as a child. Pollick soon became very proficient in his new-found interest, and is best remembered for his paintings on wagons used by the Pawnees. These small Studebaker wagons, which were assembled at the Haskell school and sent to the agency, bore his Indian portraits on the sideboards and spread-eagles on the endgates.

Art alone did not satisfy the youth, however. He took up the slide trombone, mastered it, and for several years was leader of the Haskell Institute band. He also possessed a good bass voice and sang in the chapel choir.

His talents attracted the attention of Kansas' ex-governor, Charles Robinson. Through his influence, Pollock was placed under the supervision of an artist for serious instruction.

Under this special tutorship, his attempts became more interesting and more representative of his true nature. Indian warriors in battle array and buffalo hunts, portrayed in crayon and then watercolor, composed his productions. His ability as an artist was recognized on a wider scale when some of his work was exhibited at the Smithsonian Institution in Washington.

In 1894 he completed his course at Haskell. His graduation was the occasion of a visit from his father and the Pawnee chief, Big Eagle. It was gratifying to see together the civilized son and the semi-savage father, in all his war paint and paraphernalia. Big Eagle was an ideal Indian chieftain and one of Pollock's proud admirers.

This was that difficult period when the reservations were being dissolved and Indians were taking allotments and becoming United States citizens. At age 22, Pollock took an allotment of 160 acres three miles west of the Pawnee Agency. Unlike most of the older Indians, he wholeheartedly accepted the white man's ways, obtaining employment as a clerk in the Agent's office.

One day while he was visiting the store of Finney & Sherburne, white traders at the agency, Finney handed him a piece of wrapping paper.

"Draw me a picture," the trader said.

The young artist obliged, sketching the head of Chief Big Eagle adorned with a war-bonnet.

A year later Pollock was back in Kansas, this time enrolled in the school of fine arts at the state university. His progress here was remarkable; his designs and sketches gained him no limited reputation. "In technical drawings his work is excellent," reported Professor A.H. Clark. "I am enthusiastic of his decorative ability and hope that he might continue his studies in this direction and present art history with a native American decorator."

Pollock frequently presented friends with mementoes of his work. Superintendent Peals of Haskell Institute became the proud possessor of his conception of the Messiah — a watercolor of an Indian chief in the figure of Christ standing upon the world, with uplifted hand, looking toward the clouds. On each side was an Indian brave in the attitude of prayer. Toward the group flew an eagle, the symbolic divine messenger of the Pawnee. "The picture is of value not only of its artistic merit," Peals reported, "but more because of the psychological significance which it portrays in the development of the Protestant faith."

Pollock also began conversing more freely with

acquaintances, and Professor Clark stated: "No 'society youth' was more courteous or self-possessed at class receptions than this Pawnee." On one occasion Pollock so far forgot his natural reserve as to give the entire song of the Ghost Dance, a weird chant in monotone, ending with a war-whoop which sent cold shivers down the delicate spines of his female listeners.

Pollock was compelled to leave the Kansas university because of signs of serious pulmonary trouble. When Clark asked if he intended to "return to the blanket," the Indian replied emphatically: "No, I have learned better things."

Back in the Pawnee country he took to the outdoors, riding his pony like the wind over the prairies, hoping that the dry atmosphere would soon restore his health. He was a prominent figure at all musical entertainments, and continued to paint. His specialities now were landscape and figure pieces, for which the reservation and his people were subjects and models. After a time he was appointed deputy sheriff of Pawnee County.

He was still a young man with great hopes for the future when the battleship *Maine* was sunk in Havana harbor and the United States declared war on Spain. The old courage of Pollock's fighting forebears stirred in his veins.

Although a warlike tribe, the Pawnees always had been friends and allies of the United States. For two decades they had aided the government in their eternal enmity with the Cheyenne and Sioux, who had sought to dispossess them of all the country in the upper Missouri valleys embraced by Iowa, Missouri, Kansas and Nebraska. For ten years Pawnee scouts had been employed by the government against these hostiles under the famous border military men, Major Frank North and his younger brother, Luther. Many had served in every campaign of 1864-65 and 1869-70, and won high praise for their intrepidity and soldierly efficiency.

In 1872 nearly one hundred Pawnees and their families left their reservation on the Loup Fork to hunt buffalo. They had been attacked by the Sioux and over one thousand Pawnees were massacred. The government then removed the remnants of the tribe to Indian Territory.

Following the annihilation of General George A. Custer and his command at the Little Big Horn, Major North had been dispatched to the Territory by General Phil Sheridan at Chicago to enlist the Pawnee Scouts of his old company. The army had enough men and artillery to wipe the Sioux and Cheyenne from the face of America, if it could find them. The Pawnee Scouts knew their habits and tricks of warfare; they could track them after white men had given up; and behind their skill were bitter memories of a century of suffering at the hands of the enemy.

Major North had been authorized only one hundred men, but so anxious were the Pawnees to fight that many more struggled behind on foot for two days after the quota had departed, still hoping they might be accepted.

For the Pawnee Scouts, the fall and winter campaigns of 1876 had been a series of night rides, skirmishes, escapes and surprise attacks, ending in the capture of Red Cloud's village on Chadron Creek, Nebraska, and General McKenzie's march from Crazy Woman to the Red Fork of Powder River, with defeat of the Cheyenne and their suit for peace. Major North returned to his home in Nebraska and settled down to ranching on Dismal River. The Scouts returned to the Indian Territory with many stories to tell. Their exploits while in government service had become a proud chapter in the tribe's history.

Pollock felt that he might do as well. He joined the local militia. When the call came for troops in the Spanish-American War, he was first to volunteer and led a detail of ten men from his company to Guthrie, the territorial capital, to be examined for muster into Colonel Theodore Roosevelt's Rough Riders. They were mobilized at San Antonio. Officers and men, cowboys and college graduates — wherever they came from and whatever their social positions — they possessed in common the traits of hardihood and a thirst for adventure.

In his story of the Rough Riders in *Scribner's Magazine* for January 1899, Colonel Roosevelt wrote:

The men in the ranks were mostly young. Some past their first youth had taken part in the killing of the great buffalo herds and fought Indians when the tribes were still on the warpath. The younger ones, too, had led rough lives; the lines in their faces told of many a hardship endured and many a danger silently faced with grim, unconscious philosophy. Some were originally from the East, and had seen strange adventures from sailing around the Horn to mining in Alaska. Others had been born in the West and had never seen a larger town than Santa Fe or a bigger body of water than the Pecos at flood. Some went by their own name; some had changed their names; and other possessed but half a name, like Cherokee Bill, Happy Jack, Smoky Moore, the bronco-buster, and Rattlesnake Pete, who had lived among the Moquis and taken part in the snake-dances. Some were professional gamblers, and no less than four were or had been clergymen. Some were men whose lives in the past had

55

not been free from the taint of lawlessness. A far larger number had served at different times in those bodies of armed men with which the growing civilization of the border finally puts down its savagery.

From the Indian Territory came a number of Cherokees, Chickasaws, Choctaws and Creeks. Only a few were of pure blood. The others shaded off until they were absolutely indistinguishable from their white comrades ..

Not all of the Indians were from Indian Territory (the Pawnee reservation was part of Oklahoma Territory). One of the gamest fighters and best soldiers in the regiment was Pollock, a full-blooded Pawnee. He had been educated, like most of the other Indians, at one of those admirable Indian schools which have added so much to the total of the small credit account with which the white race balances the very unpleasant debit account of its dealings with the red . . . .

Further along in his story, Roosevelt described Pollock as an excellent penman, much given to drawing pictures — "A silent, solitary fellow" whom no one would suspect of having a sense of humor.

One day the colonel was sitting in the adjutant's tent, where Pollock worked as regimental clerk, when a trooper of the First, who had been acting as a barber, entered. Eying him with immovable face, Pollock asked, in a gutteral voice, "Do you cut hair?"

"Yes," the trooper replied.

"Then," Pollock continued, "you'd better cut mine," and muttered in an explanatory soliloquy, "Don't want to wear my hair long like wild Indian when I'm in civilized war."

Pollock went into battle with the courage of his fighting ancestors, hair clipped short and without paint or war-bonnet. He was "at the front" when the Rough Riders met the Spaniards at Las Guasimas, June 24, 1898, and "still in the lead" later, when the troops fought in the hell-fire of El Poso and El Caney and dashed up San Juan Hill. Roosevelt several times commended him for personal bravery, and stated in his article: "Among the men I noticed always nearest the enemy were Pawnee Pollock, Simpson of Texas and Dudley Dean."

The only time Roosevelt ever saw a smile pass over the stoic features of this Indian was the day of mustering out at Montauk Point, New York:

> As the troops marched the commander shook hands with each of the Rough Riders. When Pollock came to him he stopped him and said: "You have been a brave and a good soldier. God bless you." It was a solemn and impressive ceremony, but a smile flitted over the Indian's face as he said good-bye.

Pollock explained afterward: "I wanted to show him my appreciation for his kind words." The smile meant more than anything the Indian could have said or done.

En route home, Pollock stopped off to visit his friends at Haskell Institute. A large reception was given in his honor. But it hardly compared to the one given him by his tribe upon arriving in Pawnee. Pollock described it in a letter to a Lawrence friend:

My oldest brother was there to receive me . . . . At the dancing ground at 8 o'clock, my half brother (Eagle Chief) welcomed me most cordially. He repeated our forefathers' motto, "Be Brave," with some of his own sayings. Next day my own brother made a feast and every warrior in camp participated. The old ones made their usual speeches, together with praise and commendations, especially to my name . . . . A young chief from Kit-Ka-Hoc band made a good speech and at the end made a present to me of a pony.

About changing my name, which is the usual custom of my tribe when a warrior returns home — this time they are at loss and cannot decide because this was a civilized war. Had I been with even one Pawnee during the campaign he might have caused my name to be changed for some certain disposition or trait while on warpath.

But if I desire new name it is easy to do. I can buy a plug of tobacco for some old Indian and during the pipe dance he will stand up before vast crowd of Indians and in his weird vocabulary repeat some ancient verse, which at the end changes my name or rather gives me a new one.

I am staying at Mud Lodge with my brother and enjoying good times . . . .

All was not well with Pollock, however. In a second letter to his Lawrence friend, in October, he stated that

I have been somewhat worried by my physical weakness that had overtaken

58

me on the train — a feeling of tired-
ness, exhaustiveness, almost like sickness. The memory of continuous moving and excitement during the campaign caused me great unrest. Now I
have been very much rested and hope
to regain my natural health . . . .

Pollock planned to return to his art study in
some eastern school. Decorative art was the
branch he wished to pursue. He also wished to
write a book of his experiences and illustrate it
himself.

In January 1899, he signed a contract with the
Buffalo Bill Wild West Show for a tour of the
country and appearances at Madison Square
Garden. He was to have joined the show in New
York City on March 21.

Pollock had survived the conflicts of Las Guasimas, El Poso, El Caney and San Juan, but could
not "throw off the evil results" contracted in the
Cuban climate. What he thought to be a trifling
fatigue and indisposition from his service with
the Rough Riders proved to be pneumonia. He
died at Pawnee March 2.

First in right of blood came the burial ceremony of his tribe. Relatives and friends gathered at the home of Eagle Chief. A mighty feast
was prepared and many speeches made, recount-
ing his daring deeds, kind acts and virtues.
Eagle Chief, as head of the Peteohawerat band,
spoke first. Expressions of deep sorrow poured
forth in the solemn Indian voice. Women wailed
and with uplifted hands called upon the Great
Father to receive the departed into the happy
hunting ground. Presents of ponies and cows
were given to the poor.

It was the custom at the death of a Pawnee to
kill his favorite pony over the grave so that he
might have it in the next world. Also all belong-

ings down to the smallest trinkets were buried with the dead. In Pollock's case, this was dispensed with, and he was buried with full military honors in Highland cemetery by the members of his old militia company, the Rough Riders and U.S. Volunteers. The G.A.R. Post furnished its flag, the first post flag to be flown at the funeral of a Rough Rider.

Theodore Roosevelt, then governor of New York, wrote Reverend J.W. Moats, who conducted the service, as follows:

I have been deeply grieved by the news of my valued comrade's death. Pollock was one of the men for whom I grew to feel the most sincere respect and liking. If possible, I would . . . have you extend my sympathy to his relatives and his fellow tribesmen, and say that he conferred honor by his conduct not only upon the Pawnee tribe, but upon the American army and nation. I wish I could have been at the funeral myself.

In November 1899, Pawnee citizens erected a handsome monument at the grave of this Indian hero and genius. The stone is three feet square at the base and twelve feet in height. Its face bears the names of William Pollock and the men who went with him from Pawnee to San Antonio.

WILLIAM POLLOCK, Pawnee Indian artist, in uniform as a Rough
Rider.

ONE OF POLLOCK'S art works exhibited at the Smithsonian Institution in Washington that won him wide recognition (cowboy roping steer on right was his conception of William F. Cody, "Buffalo Bill").

BOOK 2

"Nossah, I ain't a-feared of that little ol' specklety bull. They ain't growed a beast these ol' hands can't hold."

—Bill Pickett

4. Barehanded Bullfighter

On a sweltering afternoon in 1890, Bill Pickett, a big-handed South Texas brushpopper, swung alongside a bunch of strays he was helping bring out of the low timber country near Austin. He was riding Chico, a Roman-nosed, rawboned buckskin — "th' bes' darned cow hoss evah borned" — and the steers he was chousing from the mesquite were Mexican cattle with long, needle-pointed horns and tempered to spook at the least provocation. Some *vaqueros* brought up the rear, moving them quietly across a clearing toward the main herd.

Suddenly an old mossy-back broke from the flank and headed back to the brush. Pickett yelled to the *vaqueros:* "Stick with th' strays — I'll fetch 'im!"

He spun Chico on a hind leg and set after the steer. He didn't touch his rope — the tangled brush made it impossible to wield a lasso efficiently. Pickett had his own method of stopping a recalcitrant cow brute.

Galloping alongside, he grabbed the old mossyback by the tail, which was standing erect, took a quick dally around the saddle horn, then, by sheer strength, upended the animal in mid-air. The steer got to his feet, bellowing and shaking his head in bewilderment. Pickett trotted him in without further trouble.

"Yessah, boys," Bill explained, "when you bust 'em like that, dey sho' don't come back fo' seconds."

He grinned broadly, showing a mouthful of big white teeth. Pickett was not a big man — only 5-feet-9, with the skinny legs of a *vaquero* — but he was agile as a trapeze performer and had the broad shoulders and heavy arms of a wrestler. His *compadres* reached the herd with his performance engraved in their memories. They spread the story around their campfires and among friends on nearby ranches, and throughout the brush country Pickett became known as an expert on "tailing."

"He was nobody before that," one old-time cowman remembered. "He never even knew the date of his birth, except it happened in Williamson County, near Taylor, Texas, the year President Lincoln freed the slaves (1863). His mother was a full-blood Choctaw and his father a mixture of the white, Indian and African races. He spent his boyhood as a ranch hand around Taylor, Round Rock and Georgetown, then worked down on the Rio Grande until 1890. He grew up with Mexicans and learned to ride and rope with the best of them."

By accident he stumbled onto the trick that made him world famous and evolved into today's most rugged and popular rodeo contest event — "bulldogging," or steer wrestling.

Some time after the "tailing" incident, he was working with a cowboy who used a big yellow mastiff to bring unruly cattle out of the dense overgrowths of mesquite trees, low bushes with long thorns, briars, and greasebushes so matted and intertwined it was almost impossible for man or horse to penetrate. Some old lean, rough longhorns, which the cowboy considered "loco in the head," would worm their way into these thickets to feed on the mesquite beans and briar leaves. The cowboy would ride to the edge of the thickets, listening for any cattle movement. Beside him trotted his bulldog, Spike. Spike had been trained to go into these bramble traps and bring out strays by any means possible — nipping their heels, or barking in front of them, making the old "briar-pushers" charge him, foot by foot, as he gradually backed into a clearing.

When old cows were caught in the entangling briars and without food and water became too weak to make an effort to escape, the bulldog would give them the added incentive to free themselves. If that didn't work, the cowboy would chop his way to the rescue with a sharp hatchet, carried as part of his equipment, rather than leave them to the mercy of the wolves, mountain lions and rattlesnakes.

Spike seemed to anticipate with high excitement his role of rescuer. Once he had his victim in the clear, he would sink his strong teeth into the nerve tender upper lip of the brute. The cow would shake her head viciously a few times, flinging the dog back and forth like a pendulum. Finally, the intense pain caused by the weight of the dog's body brought her down with a thud.

Then the cowboy would rope or doctor her as necessary. Once released, she made for the open prairie. One or two encounters with Spike always made these critters leave the thickets to the varmints.

Bill was thinking of Spike the day he went after a longhorn cow that had a young calf hidden in a thicket. The cow was a smart old "busher." Pickett knew that if he followed her she would lead him away from the calf, so he rode the opposite direction until he saw where she was headed, then took after her. The calf sighted him, jumped up and ran to the side of its mother, tail high and bawling.

The cow began bawling too. Weak from calving and a long winter, she refused to leave the thicket. She faced Bill, on the prod and fighting mad.

Pickett loosened his catch rope. Unable to swing it, he tossed it underhanded from his horse.

The cow charged, head down and hooking at Chico's belly. Bill leaned out and grabbed a horn to keep his favorite mount from being gored. The cow pulled him from the saddle, dragging him through the thicket. Bill's frightened horse ran off, leaving him alone with the cow.

As Pickett told it later,

> I held on tight. I knew if I let go, we'd have a foot race. An' I nevah was fast on my feet. I got my left arm under th' other horn an' twisted her nose to'ard the sky, fo'cing her neck back to bust her down. I sho' was mad at that darned cow fo' tryin' to hurt my Chico .

Chico dashed back to the "gather," and some of the hands rode in search of Pickett while he wrestled the enraged cow. Finally resorting to Spike's method of subduing steers, Pickett socked his big teeth into the cow's upper lip. The old longhorn came crashing down on her side.

> That's how th' boys found me — arms locked ovah bofe horns an' still bitin' th' cow's muzzle with my teeth. Th' boss rode up, an' remarked, "Bill, you're holdin' that cow like a bulldog." He throwed his rope, an' I put it 'round her head. "Turn 'er loose, Bill," he said, "she can't get you now."
>
> Well, she got up an' charged me. But th' rope stopped her. Then th' boys went to work with their ropes, an' dey soon had her an' th' calf out of the mesquite.
>
> It was while ridin' back to th' herd that I got th' idea of jumpin' from my hoss to cattle's head an' horns, catchin' an' throwin' 'em with my teeth like old Spike, as it wouldn't cut up th' stock like that bulldog did.

In 1893, while working for Lee Moore near Rockdale, Pickett watched a group of cowmen attempting to drive a bunch of wild steers into the railroad stock pens to ship them to Kansas City. In the assembly were such old-timers as Billy Brown, Morgan Lewis and Frate Parker.

Pickett laughed when several steers got away. "I can catch 'em with my teeth," he commented.

"Let him try it," Brown retorted.

Before the words left his mouth, a big three-year-old broke from the drive.

"Stop him, Bill," Lee Moore shouted.

"Yessah!"

Pickett turned Chico so fast he almost "lost his saddle." A few good jumps and Chico had his rider's legs crowding the rump of the Chihuahua longhorn and turning him back to the pens.

At the same instant, seemingly without effort, Pickett leaped to the head of the steer. Chico kept running, pulling Bill's feet forward as he got the neck-and-horn hold and dropping him down the steer's side. Bill dug his heels in the earth to bring the animal to a halt. A quick twist of the horns brought the steer's nose upward in reach of Bill's teeth, and he clamped down with all his might, throwing his full weight on the brute's nostrils. After a lunge or two the steer flopped over on his side. Then Pickett threw both hands in the air as a signal for Lee Moore to come help.

Moore and Brown rode up. Moore cut the steer away as Pickett leaped to his feet. Brown, a brave man who had never ventured closer to a wild longhorn than the length of his lariat, sat his mount, slack-jawed and staring.

"Bill, you black rascal!" he exclaimed. "That was some stunt!"

A few months later Pickett performed the feat again near the stock pens at Hempstead, in Waller County, catching and throwing three steers in succession.

Following these incidents, bulldogging with him became a sport. Lee Moore took him to various events around the country. Every time Bill threw a steer with his teeth, the crowd stood up and roared. Rodeos in those days were little more than picnics or "cowboy contests," as they were called, held by cattlemen for their own amusement. One rancher would furnish the broncs, another the cattle, a third the saddle horses. All chipped in on the expenses and prize money, which at most usually totaled less than $100. Local merchants furnished the fence for the pens and arena. Since everyone in the community contributed, they didn't feel like charging admission. They were not showmen, so knew nothing of publicity to draw outsiders. These contests, however, soon became something more than private affairs.

Pickett appeared at every Texas event from San Angelo to Houston. Then Lee Moore arranged for him to bulldog in public at a Confederate reunion in Nashville, Tennessee. This led to other engagements at Tucson and Phoenix, Arizona.

At Phoenix, Jack Gibson, a prominent sports-minded citizen, after witnessing a Pickett demonstration, secured the use of Eastlake Park and advertized widely. This western exhibition drew an immense crowd of local residents, out-of-town cowboys, ranchers and farmers. The spectators, many of whom had come to razz Pickett, stared in disbelief and then cheered while he downed ten steers and broke a dozen "rough-string" broncs brought in from nearby ranches.

From there, Moore took him to Colorado and the fair at Grand Forks, North Dakota. After that, Bill left Lee Moore, and Dave McClure, "Mr. Cowboy" himself, took Bill and towed him all over the country wherever there was a big contest or frontier celebration. He was billed in the newspapers as the most daring cowboy alive — "The Dusky Demon."

70

"And now, ladies and gentlemen," the announcer would call, and the cry became as familiar across the land as the "soooey" of the farmer summoning pigs to the trough, "you are about to witness the amazing Bill Pickett, *throwing a ferocious longhorn with his teeth!*"

Foghorn Clancy, whose spectacular voice in 1898 started him on a career as rodeo announcer, promoter and handicapper and carried him the next fifty years to almost every rodeo, round-up and stampede in North America, saw the dusky cowboy bulldog for the first time at Dublin, Texas, at the turn of the century. "The stunt was considered then, and for years afterward, the most daring trick performed by a human being," he said.

Harold T. Mapes, Wyoming rancher and rodeo veteran, who rode with Pickett in 1905, stated that

> as far as I know no white man ever copied his act. Few had the nerve to try. It was going a little too far for a decent cowhand to take a mouthful of snotty upper lip of a lousy critter. It used to turn my stomach. But Bill always got a roar or applause from the audience.
>
> No cow, bull or steer ever tried to hook Bill after a "bulldogging." Sometimes Bill would get up, paw dirt like an angry critter, and bellow. The animal would shudder, leap to its feet, and head for the nearest exit.

At Fort Worth this same year, the bulldogger was spotted by Colonel Joe Miller, one of the three owners of the fabulous 101 Ranch in Oklahoma that combined cattle, farming and oil interests and bankrolled a lively Wild West show

71

and circus that made even the Ringling Brothers take notice. Colonel Miller immediately contracted Pickett to appear with the show. Offered steady employment, a home, and work for any of his children who were old enough, Bill moved his family to Oklahoma, and for the next thirty years, he was practically a protege of the Miller brothers — Joe, Zack and George.

At the 101, Pickett renewed his acquaintance with some of the top hands he had met at contests across the country — Kurt Reynolds and Johnny Brewer, "two of th' best bronc-busters evah," and Jim Hopkins, who, drunk or sober, "could do anything with a rope 'cept picture drawin'."

Will Rogers was among the 101 bunch. He was never on the ranch payroll, but for nearly five years he had been drifting over from the Cherokee Nation, staying weeks at a time "to be with th' boys." In 1901, he and Zack Miller had attended Buffalo Bill's Wild West show at Guthrie, and Will became so excited over the antics of a Mexican maguey artist named Vicenzo Orapeza that he stayed through the second performance. On the way back to the ranch, he told Zack: "A year from now I'll be doing anything that Mexican did — or wear out every rope on the reservation."

Rogers did just that, and kept on doing it, from Madison Square Garden to the Ziegfeld Follies, and right up to the day of the plane crash in Alaska that killed him and Wiley Post. On the 101, he used one of Pickett's sons to help in his practice. He would have the boy ride past "hell-bent for election," then set his loops whirling, and "dab 'em on whatever foot th' boy called out."

Tom Mix was in the bunch, too. A former bartender in Oklahoma City and Guthrie, Tom learned to ride and rope on the 101. But his main job was spinning windies to tenderfeet about the ranch's wild and bloody history. "He could color a story redder than a Navajo blanket," Zack Miller said, "and told his scary tales so often he got to believing them himself — especially the one about his being half Indian." Actually, Tom was a mixture of French-Canadian and Italian. Handsome, prettied up in fancy cowboy garb and saddle rigging, he was a natural before cranking movie cameras in Southern California and became king of the silent Westerns.

The stage and screen never appealed to Pickett as it did to Mix and Rogers. Pickett achieved his fame in the sweat and dust of the rodeo and Wild West show arena. For the next decade, "The Dusky Demon" blossomed on the front pages from Portland, Maine to Portland, Oregon. But his "biggest thrill," Bill remembered, was the first time he bulldogged in Madison Square Garden. He had long since retired his old buckskin Chico, and that night he was riding his new "war-hoss," a little bay pony named Spradley.

Spradley had been an orphan colt, whose mother had fallen with her rider in a drift of snow trying to turn a herd of cattle the winter before Bill came to the 101. Her leg had been broken and the muscles deep in her upper shoulder laid bare by a splintered tree limb. The Millers had been forced to kill her. When Colonel Joe offered Bill his choice of a mount, Bill had picked that lonely little fellow — her colt. His hair was shiny and his mane and tail full and glossy. He already was old enough to ride, but he had jumped a corral fence and run a pine splinter into his brisket. A tumor had formed, the size of Bill's fist. Still, he could outrun any colt on the range. Bill had cut out the tumor, cured the colt and gentled and trained him until he was "th' best bulldoggin' hoss in my string."

When Colonel Joe asked why he had named

the colt Spradley, Bill explained, "Well, suh, he always runs so fast he takes all fo' feet off de ground at once, an' his hind feet look like dey has to *spraddle* to go 'round th' front ones 'fore he hits th' ground agin."

Bill always was proud to show off Spradley's quick getaway, quick stop, ability to turn on a dime. And when he cantered the horse into Madison Square Garden that night in the Grand Entrance Parade, if he had been riding in a diamond-studded chariot, he couldn't have been happier.

Tom Mix, clad in his flashiest, god-of-the-prairie raiment, went up in the boxes among the Long Island and Westchester society to tell his bloody tales of the *true* West. Bill backed his horse up on one side of the chute, fixing to do his bulldogging act. His hazer sashayed to the opposite side into position.

Bill quieted Spradley down and gave the chute man the nod. The gate flew open, and into the arena lunged Bill's steer.

All that was on the old longhorn's mind when he quit the chute was to head back to Texas. Horrified by New York's bright lights and the sea of faces around him, he lit for the fence in a cloud of dust like he had sprouted wings. Spradley couldn't catch him, and the top boards of the high gate to the first balcony didn't stop him. The rising aisle of steps beyond seemed the only avenue of escape — he had climbed steeper ridges through the *huisache* thickets along the Nueces river — and he took them four at a jump, wringing his tail and roaring like a tornado.

But the old *ladino* hadn't got away yet. Bill raked his spurs against Spradley's flanks, cleared the fence and headed up after him. The hazer, kicking his mount over the splintered pine barrier and rope spinning above his head like an enlarged angel's circlet, brought up the rear.

74

The crowd was on its feet, screaming. Women fainted. News photographers fumbled for flasks of flash powder. The steer reached the second balcony, still wringing his tail and roaring. And down in the arena, the announcer, trying to prevent a stampede, lied at the top of his lungs: "Keep your seats folks! There's not the slightest danger!"

As the steer slammed into the third balcony, Pickett jumped to his head and horns. The crash, as Bill and the steer hit the floor, shook the grandstand. The hazer flipped his lariat the same instant, and the loop snapped around the steer's threshing heels.

The hazer turned his horse back down the steps, bumping Bill and the steer behind him. By the time the trio reached the sawdust again, $50 silk hats and ladies muffs were showering them like confetti. The balconies howled, and smoke from the photographers' flash powder rose in a black cloud to the Garden's roof. The next afternoon New York newspapers plastered the story across their pages, and no one had the faintest idea that the feat they had witnessed had not been part of an act.

For the six remaining days of the show, Bill packed them in. He didn't bulldog any more steers in the grandstand, but he always brought his audience to its feet.

He was lauded by thousands at the Jamestown Exposition in 1907. Then he bulldogged through the Middle West, up to St. Paul, through Wisconsin, and to Winnipeg, Canada. In one afternoon the show made $7,500. At Calgary, on Dominion Day, the crowds were so large that some of the meanest animals had to be pulled out of the acts to keep them from trampling the spectators.

Pickett bulldogged day and night. Sometimes he would miss getting that tooth-hold. When he

75

did, he would just "peg" his steer (shove the left horn in the ground and let him roll rump-over-head). It was still a feat to take a man's breath, and took the same guts, strength and timing.

Nor did he confine his reckless daring to wild cattle. One of his best performances was bull-dogging a buffalo. Bill knew that a buffalo's neck wasn't made to wrestle him down with; he knocked the animal down more by momentum than by his great strength.

He never failed to respond with grinning alacrity to the challenge of the rough and ready westerners who vowed he could not subdue this man-killing critter or another. At El Paso, they pitted him against a furious elk with a tremendous sweep of snaggy, bladed horns and strong enough in its forefeet to have killed him with one stroke. Pickett wrestled and threw the huge animal in less than ten minutes and emerged unscathed.

The Millers believed the four-footed, herbivorous beast that could beat him in a standup fight had not been born, and with this conviction, they invaded Mexico.

They unloaded the show at Mexico City the night before Guadalupe Day, 1908. The Mexican capital was jammed. Next morning, thousands of worshippers climbed the nearby heights to pay respects to their favorite saint, then came down to see what the Americans had to offer.

The show paraded down *Paseo de la Reforma*. Mexico's president, Porfirio Diaz, came down to the second performance and brought his brother's grandchildren. The children liked the show clowns. They would set the dogs on them, and the clowns would climb the tent poles to keep from being bitten. This pleased Diaz. He gave the show his approval. But it did not improve the mediocre attendance.

The show's press agent worked on *El Heraldo,*

the city's leading newspaper, for publicity. Senor Louis F. Correa, of the *Herald,* was sympathetic, but not enthusiastic. The riding and roping acts were not new to the Mexicans. Pickett's mid-air leap from the saddle to the flying horns of his quarry, his struggle for supremacy and inevitable overturning of the animal, was the only American performance worthy of comparison with their own beloved bullfighting. The bullfighters, who came in a group one afternoon to witness the exhibition, laughed contemptuously and stated they could do even that, as well and in less time.

Joe Miller knew the difficulty of the feat. He immediately offered one thousand pesos to any member of the proud fraternity who had the nerve to duplicate it.

Bienvenida, noted for his eye and stroke, and as deadly a matador as Mexico ever produced, accepted the challenge. He could not perform in public — it would be unethical and a disgrace to the art — but he would appear privately, with representatives of the press as witnesses, promptly at 10 o'clock the next morning, "to teach the boasting *Americanos* a lesson in grace and courage!"

The stage was set. The witnesses arrived. But Bienvenida failed to show, and sent no word of explanation.

Joe Miller sent a messenger to his hotel. There lolled Bienvenida, rather shamefaced and regretful. He had been forbidden by bull-ring officials to risk his valuable neck outside the national arena!

Joe went to the *Herald* office and placed an advertisement, challenging any *two* bullfighters of Mexico to come into the show ring and throw *one* steer in the same time Pickett was throwing *three.*

This offer wasn't accepted, either.

Joe should have been content with his moral triumph. But his Americanism was running rampant. He publicly charged the fraternity with showing the white feather. "Mexico ain't growed a beast Bill Pickett can't hold," he boasted, then announced that his man, barehanded and without assistance, would grasp by the horns the most blood-hungry bull the Republic could provide and stay in the arena for fifteen minutes, spending at least five on the bull's head — for the gate receipts and $5,000. And Pickett hadn't even been consulted!

He did not bet that Pickett could throw the animal—he knew that the necks of these bulls, like buffalo, were too thick for them to be twisted down. Joe, however, was not familiar with bull-ring procedure. The *muleta,* which the bull was taught from infancy to detest, was the object of attack. The matador evaded his mad rushes, never grappled. He did not dare lay hands on the beast.

That Miller's cowboy would engage such an animal in hand-to-hand combat was, to the Mexican mind, apparent superlative folly. The dumfounded bullfighters and their worshippers covered the bet eagerly, and the bull-ring officials agreed. They were certain the bull — if Pickett succeeded in getting his hands on him — would shake the cowboy loose in a natter of seconds and gore him to death.

Senor Rivero, impresario of *Plaza del Toro,* the new concrete and steel arena, promptly gave permission to hold the encounter there, and Joe delegated him to select the animal. Rivero chose *Chiquita Frijole* (Little Bean).

Little Bean was a beautiful animal, almost purple in color, with darker, bean-sized speckles over his body. No old brush-wild, proddy Texas longhorn, Pickett realized the moment he saw him. This was a fighting bull, wary and wicked,

bred and reared for the ring on the famous
Tepeyahualeo granaderia. Already he had taken
the lives of two men and a half dozen horses, but
had been spared the death thrust upon the en-
treaties of spectators. So fierce and strong a bull,
they cried, ought not suffer an inglorious death.
Little Bean had been returned to the corrals,
where he now waited, pawing the ground and
bellowing his unabated longing to kill. He held
his head high and proud, sharp horns set for
hooking.

"Think you can handle him, Bill?" Joe asked,
wondering now if he had overestimated the bulldogger's ability.

Pickett held up his black hands of steel. "Like
you said, Colonel Joe, they ain't growed a beast
these ol' hands can't hold."

But that night he appeared at Miller's tent,
shifting his hat in his hands.

Joe's eyes searched the bulldogger's face. "You
change your mind, Bill?"

"Nossah," Pickett replied. "I ain't a-feared of
that little ol' specklety bull. It's jus' that a man's
time has gotta come sooner or later. I may be
doggin' a bull or bustin' a bronc. Maybe this is
my time, maybe it ain't. But if'n it is, I wants to
know if I can be put away amongst my friends."

"We'll bury you on the 101," Joe promised.

"In the hard ground, where the coyotes can't
scratch out my bones?"

"In the hard ground, Bill."

Pickett's face broke in a wide grin. "Thank
you, Colonel. I'se ready fo' that little ol' specklety
bull now." He left the tent, still grinning.

Nearly 25,000 persons, the largest crowd ever
to stream through the gates of *Plaza del Toro,*
turned out to see the cowboy "sacrifice himself
upon the altar of American egotism." They came
from every direction — in carriages, on horseback and afoot — a gay, colorful people teeming

79

with the expectancy of the hour. Women were dressed in their finest Parisian gowns and jewelry. Senoritas in their lace *mantillas* decorated the railing of their boxes with brilliant Spanish shawls, the fringes rippling in the breeze. Cavaliers appeared groomed to perfection, and President Diaz and other ranking officials added dignity to the occasion. Gate receipts for the day totaled $48,000, making the total wager $53,000.

The show troupe, fourteen-hundred strong, escorted Pickett to the arena. Senor Rivero and Senor Bravo, *presidente,* received them with apprehension. Obviously they had expected the cowboy to lose courage at the last moment.

Actually, Pickett was never more confident and eager for a fray. As Joe Miller said afterward, "He was ready to spit in Death's eye."

Joe had planned a few preliminary acts to give the crowd its money's worth. But the crowd wasn't interested in bronc and trick riding. The Mexicans booed the performers and set up a chant for their favorite bull. *"Viva el toro!"* they yelled. *"Viva el Chiquita Frijole!"*

Then an uninvited, gruesome spectacle appeared in the arena — some bullfighters carrying a black coffin. Printed on the outside was *El Pincharino,* meaning a man who has been riddled by the horns of a bull.

"El Pincharino! El Pincharino!" the Mexicans screamed. The lust for blood and battle was upon them. The stands shook with the thunder of sound.

Joe rode to the announcer's booth. "Might as well call everything off and let them have it," he said.

The arena was cleared. The performers retired behind the barriers, and the *Gran Lucha Taurina-Humana* was announced. A vast silence fell over the crowd. Then into the ring dashed Pickett on Spradley.

Bill had been coached in proper entrance. He rode directly to the President's box. There were boos and hisses. He wasn't dressed in the flashing tinsel and gold embroidery of the bullfighter. He wore a coarse blue shirt and Levi's. But he had on a good pair of bench-made boots and a white Five-X Beaver Stetson — all that a cowboy needed to be dressed up. He lifted his Stetson and reared Spradley on his hind legs in a courteous salute, then rode out to wait for the bull.

Timbers cracked and rattled in a chute on the far side of the ring. *Picadores,* mounted on worthless horses, were stabbing the bull with their barbed darts and lances, working him into a frenzy. Then someone threw in a bundle of fireworks. There was a nasty explosion and crackling, the chute opened, and *Chiquita Frijoli,* his glossy hide scorched and bleeding, jumped high and bellowing into the arena, tossing his horns and searching for his tormentors.

The crowd cheered. Here was their favorite bull to put those bragging *Americanos* in their places! *Chiquita Frijole* sighted Pickett astride his little bay horse and came on the run, horns lowered for the kill.

Spradley had put Bill alongside too many bulls not to know their moods and ways. He knew that a bull closed his eyes when he charged and a Texas longhorn didn't.

The crowd came to its feet. It seemed impossible that those horns should miss. When the sharp points were only a few feet away, Spradley jumped swiftly aside. As the bull swept past, he planted his hind hoofs solidly against the beast's ribs.

The momentum carried the bull several yards, but he spun and charged back so quickly there was no time for a second defense. He caught the little bay squarely behind, with such force the horns drove all the way into the thick muscles of his rump. Whinnying in pain, Spradley sank down in the rear. As the bull withdrew for another lunge, Pickett went out of the saddle over the horse's tail. He landed astraddle the bull's head, between the blood-smeared horns, and grasped him beneath the neck.

This was the moment awaited by the spectators. The wonderfully lithe and agile cowboy, experts had conceded, might secure a hold on the bull, but never, they had declared, could he keep it for half a minute. One toss of the head would dislodge him, and in a matter of seconds, his "guts would be ripped from his body." *Plaza del Toro* became a cage of howling maniacs.

For a couple of minutes, the speckled, tormented devil made a whip-cracker out of Bill Pickett. He swung his head high and from side to side, trying to fling Bill free. He slammed the cowboy into the arena wall. He even rammed his head against the ground in an attempt to drag Bill loose.

Dust boiled and rolled. The hot, rank scent of the maddened animal and the smell of fresh blood — Spradley's blood — reeked in Bill's nostrils. There was no time for fancy bite-'em-on-the-lip bulldogging. This was a battle to the finish. And no one knew it better than Pickett.

He remained glued like a leech, one arm over each horn, big hands clamped like a vice on the bull's throat, and his powerful knees squeezing the bull's nostrils, cutting off the much needed air.

In another three minutes the cowboy had the beast tottering on his feet. The haughty, shaggy head was aslant under the force exerted upon his nostrils and throat by the swinging man.

Bill's lips peeled in a white-toothed grin, but there was no mirth in it. He was aware that his five minutes were up, but the Mexican timekeeper had refused to stop the clock so that Miller's cowboys could ride in, rope the bull and spread him. The crowd had become an inflamed mob.

Angry shouts of *"Viva! Viva el toro!"* swept the grandstand. Someone cried in Spanish: "Remember Bienvenida!" — as if Pickett had stabbed him in the back — and a cushion was hurled at the cowboy's head.

Someone threw a jagged stone, and crimson streamed down Bill's cut face. Then hell broke loose. The crowd shouted insults and howled for his blood. Fruits, bottles, canes and knives showered the cowboy as he battled for his life, and no one lifted a finger to stop it. Bill looked up into the hate of the crowd, and his eyes filled with tears.

The show troupe appealed to the police. The police only laughed. So they pleaded with Miller for permission to retaliate with American cartridges, but Joe realized that could only result in wholesale extermination. Ten minutes passed — fifteen. Their hats were reeking with expectorations from the human brutes above the barrier.

The bull passed them again. Pickett was weakening fast, his face turned gray from strain. Sheer courage was all that kept him hanging on. He tried to work the bull toward the barricade, hoping to turn loose and reach safety ahead of those needle-pointed horns.

Joe snapped his watch shut and turned to a cowboy, Ves Pegg. "Them bastards ain't going to ring that bell, Ves," he said. "They aim to let that bull kill old Bill. Strip off your shirt!

"Now, the moment Bill lets go, get over that wall. Wave your garment as close to the bull as you dare, and see if you can save your comrade's life!"

The order came none too soon. A brick hurled from the stands struck Pickett in the side, cracking two ribs. With a groan and a last, imploring look at his companions, he released his grip on the bull. *Chiquita Frijole* lowered his horns for the death thrust . . . .

Over the barrier leaped the half-naked Ves Pegg. The bull glimpsed it even before the astonished spectators — the hated moving garment being brandished almost in his face. For a moment he hesitated, then leaped across Pickett and charged the insolent cowboy.

Pegg beat him to the wall easily. Pickett crawled to his feet and staggered to the barricade in time for Miller and the others to haul him to safety.

Later, Pickett returned to salute the President. More bricks, bottles and *machete* knives came whizzing down at him. But Bill wouldn't have cared if they had been firing bullets. He took his time leading his crippled horse from the arena.

"Muerte al Pincharino! Kill the black man!" came the cry from the stands. "Kill *all* the American dogs!"

The crowd came surging down to reach the bulldogger and show troupe that had brought them shame. But Diaz, reading the tragedy-rife atmosphere, had ordered up a troop of *rurales*. Quickly they formed an escort corridor of loaded rifles and drawn sabers and led the Miller party back to their grounds. Without this assistance, the entire troupe might have been slaughtered and Pickett lynched.

There were demonstrations in the city that night, but the Mexican hatred soon abated. Miller collected his $53,000 and returned the show to the United States, "with the patriotic satisfaction of knowing all Mexico could not put forward a man so intrepidly brave as Oklahoma's half-breed gladiator."

The southern Republic angrily discussed the event for a quarter century afterward, and the 101 Ranch became one of the top tourist attractions in the world. Its famed White House played host to thousands from all walks of life — queens, presidents and foreign diplomats to common cowboys. Twice its Wild West shows toured England and Europe, and Bill Pickett performed before the crowned heads of five continents.

As time passed, bite-'em-on-the-lip bulldogging went out of fashion. In many places in the United States, and abroad, it was banned as "cruelty to dumb animals." Bill, on more than one occasion, was arrested and fined. By the early 1920s, the sport had been reduced to plain steer wrestling.

Pickett took the change in stride. The years were creeping up on him. Numerous bones in his body had been broken, and he had lost all his front teeth from "biting the steer."

Spradley's wounds had healed. Bill never used him to bulldog after his Mexican adventure, but following his acts, he would always remount the little bay horse and ride him into the arena to accept the applause.

After Joe Miller died in 1926 and George Miller was killed in an automobile accident eighteen months later, the great 101 Ranch began to crumble. Pickett obtained a section of land near Chandler, Oklahoma, to become a modest rancher, but he wasn't content away from the old life. His wife had died and his children married. He returned to the 101 in 1932. He was nearly 70.

Zack Miller was sick in bed, and the property plastered with mortgages and threatened foreclosures. Zack owned some horses that weren't subject to auction and wanted them cut from the herd. Bill agreed to do the job for him.

A big sorrel in the bunch kept dodging back to the far corner of the corral. Pickett finally dabbed on his loop, and the horse plunged and fell over backwards. Pickett hauled him to his feet. As the animal stood dazed a moment, Bill started up the rope, hand over hand, toward him.

Pickett must have known the danger of this position. Perhaps his mind was on his sick friend.

The horse snorted and reared high, chopping with his forefeet. Bill dodged back, too late. The deadly hammer blows struck him in the chest and head.

He lived only eleven days after the horse pawed him. On the date of his death, April 2, 1932, Zack Miller wrote this touching obituary:

Old Bill has died and gone away,
Over the "Great Divide."
Gone to a place where the preachers say
Both saint and sinner will abide.
If they "check his brand" like I think they will
It's a runnin' hoss they'll give to Bill
And some good wild steers till he gets his fill
With a great big crowd for him to thrill.
Bill's hide was black but his heart was white
To help a "doggie" in a dyin' fight
To save a dollar for his boss.
And all Bill wanted was a good fast hoss,
Three square meals and a place to lay
His tired self at the end of day.
There's one other thing, since I've come to think,
Bill was always willing to take a drink.
If the job was tough, be it hot or cold,
You could get it done if Bill was told.
He'd fix the fence, or skin a cow,
Or ride a bronc, and EVEN PLOW,
Or do anything, if you told him how.
Like many men in the old-time West,
On any job, he did his best.
He left a blank that's hard to fill
For there'll never be another Bill.
Both White and Black will mourn the day
That the "Biggest Boss" took Bill away.

BILL PICKETT on his "war-hoss" Spradley.

BILL PICKETT (studio pose), Choctaw-Negro cowboy who invented today's most rugged and popular rodeo contest event — "bulldogging," or
steer wrestling.

COLONEL JOE MILLER of the fabulous 101 Ranch of Oklahoma, who
spotted Pickett at Fort Worth in 1905 and offered him life-time work on
the ranch and in its Wild West show.

BILL PICKETT demonstrating his "bite-'em-on-the-lip" method of bull-dogging a Texas longhorn.

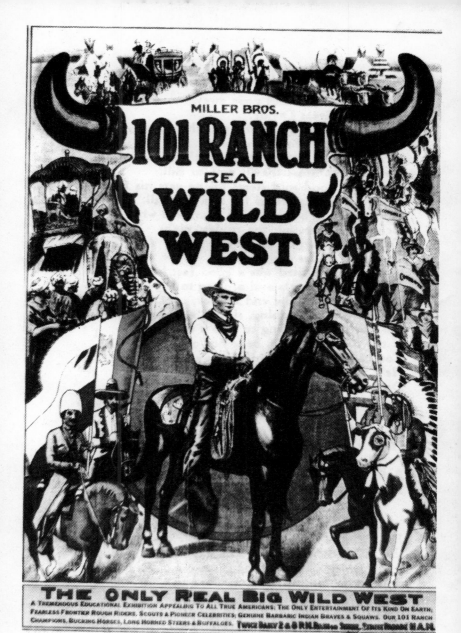

AN EARLY PIECE of the Miller Brothers' 101 Ranch Real Wild West Show advertising. Bill Pickett became one of the show's greatest attractions.

OLD BILL IS DEAD

Old Bill has died and gone away,
Over the "Great Divide."
Gone to a place where the preachers say
Both saint and sinner will abide.
If they "check his brand" like I think they will
It's a runnin' hoss they'll give to Bill.
And some good wild steers till he gets his fill.
With a great big crowd for him to thrill.
Bill's hide was black but his heart was white,
He'd sit up through the coldest night
To help a "doggie" in a dyin' fight,
To save a dollar for his boss.
And all Bill wanted was a good fast hoss,
Three square meals and a place to lay
His tired self at the end of day,
There's one other thing, since I've come to think,
Bill was always willing to take a drink.
If the job was tough, be it hot or cold,
You could get it done if Bill was told.
He'd fix the fence, or skin a cow,
Or ride a bronc, and EVEN PLOW,
Or do anything, if you told him how.
Like many men in the old-time West,
On any job, he did his best.
He left a blank that's hard to fill
For there'll never be another Bill.
Both White and Black will mourn the day
That the "Biggest Boss" took Bill away.

———

"Bill" Pickett was born about 1860; died April 2, 1932, from injuries received while roping a bronc on the 101 Ranch. He was the originator of that great rodeo sport, "bulldogging", having been the first man to jump from his horse onto the head of a running steer.

This was written on the day of his death by one who had been his boss for thirty years.

—Z. T. Miller

PICKETT OBITUARY written by Colonel Zack Miller on date of the bull-dogger's death, April 2, 1932.

His funeral was conducted on the front gallery of the White House, and they buried him, as Colonel Joe had promised, in the hard ground on the 101, on a high ridge in the buffalo pasture south of Marland called Cowboy Hill. On September 6, 1936, the far-famed Cherokee Strip Cowpunchers' Association erected a stone marker at his grave.

At Oklahoma City, on December 9, 1971, in a ceremony at the State Fairgrounds Arena during the National Finals Rodeo, Bill Pickett became the first black cowboy to be enshrined in the National Rodeo Hall of Fame of the National Cowboy Hall of Fame and Western Heritage Center.

5. Lasso Genius

Much has been written about trick and fancy roping in nearly a century spanning the beginning of Wild West shows to today's rodeos — even unbelievable reputations have been given some practitioners of this cowboy art. But historians of the era, somehow, have neglected Jose Berrara, known as "Mexican Joe," who was one of the greatest ropers of them all.

One of the first in the Wild West business, Mexican Joe, taught many of the early Western motion picture stars the technique of the *maguey* and *reata,* and did as much as any man to make rodeos entertaining and respectable. He achieved a world-wide reputation, and for forty years his attainments went undisputed and unchallenged. In his best days, he roped as many as six horses or four buffalo running abreast in the arena.

He was born at San Antonio, Texas, May 10, 1876. The Berreras were one of the prominent and well-to-do Spanish families, many of whom were direct descendants of the Canary Island colonists. They were the old Spanish aristocracy of the town. But Jose spent his formative years on the hurricane decks of mustang ponies in the cow camps along the Rio Grande, and roping wild cattle from the brush on the family ranch in Mexico.

In 1897, Major Gordon W. Lillie (Pawnee Bill) went into winter quarters at Frederick, Maryland, with his Historical Wild West and Indian Encampment, which he had put on the road ten years earlier, and as always, he added new features and personalities. While picking up some show stock that Jose delivered to him at San Antonio, he was struck by the youth's dashing appearance on his red-eyed steed, replete with brass trimmed accouterments of elaborately carved leather. He was more impressed by the youth's skill in handling livestock and his accuracy with a lariat. Before Lillie left San Antonio, he signed Jose as a member of his troupe. In native regalia and trappings, Jose became "Mexican Joe," chief of *vaqueros,* and for the next fifteen years, while the show toured Europe and North America, he was one of its top attractions.

Joe's favorite story was the time in 1908 when the combined Pawnee Bill and Buffalo Bill shows opened in Madison Square Garden and Will Rogers, soon to become the country's best known humorist, would come down in the afternoons to visit with the cowboys and ride in the parades. Between performances, he and Joe would get out their lariats and practice different "throws" and "catches." Rogers especially liked the Big Horse Catch, and Joe taught him to rope five horses running abreast.

One evening, Joe and his cowboys were Rogers' "honorable guests" at a "swell dinner party." Rogers got off to one side and sat cross-legged on the floor. Joe and his boys followed suit. Rogers began cracking jokes. Everybody was laughing "fit to kill" and having some drinks.

Joe noticed that Rogers wasn't drinking, so he asked, "Bill, how come?" Rogers reached out and gathered several empty bottles from among the boys, and said, "Why, look at these, Joe!" Joe chuckled, "Reckon I was wrong, Bill."

Barrera would conclude his story: "Rogers never was much of a drinker, but he certainly was a top hand at spinning yarns and a loop."

The rope was used for catching livestock long before the American West was forming its glamorous traditions, but the cowboy was the first to master it and make it perform incredible tricks. "Roping fever," as old cowmen called it, ruined many a good cowhand. Clement Van Rogers, prominent rancher in the Cherokee Nation, once complained about his son Will being no good for anything except spinning a lariat. But that was before the things Will had to say made him one of the most beloved men of his time. Years later, Will asked himself: "Has anybody that has ever become afflicted with trick roping ever been cured of it? When? How? Where?"

What these old cowmen failed to appreciate was the appeal to the imagination that comes from the graceful, rhythmic floating of a well-handled *maguey* and the constant challenge to master the many variations of the Wedding Ring, the Merry-go-round, the Butterfly, the Skip, the Juggle, the Hurdler, the Skyrocket, the Crinoline, and the intricacies of hundreds of other spins and tricks.

Unlike Rogers and other ropers, it was not Joe's tricks with the hemp that made him the hero of the show world. It was his bold courage to dab a loop on anything with four legs.

He received his first national publicity with the Pawnee Bill show in Washington, D.C., when an elephant broke from the zoo and roamed the capitol streets, treeing a number of citizens. Mexican Joe mounted his red-eyed pony, threw a Figure 8 over the front and hind feet of the huge pachyderm and detained him until the keepers arrived. Joe called his catch a *figura ocho*.

On another occasion, in New York City, a lion escaped from the Ringling Brothers' Circus. Joe tossed a Johnny Blocker loop on the King of the Jungle and escorted the beast out of the frightened crowd back to its cage.

His best known exploit occurred during a show parade down State Street hill in Albany. The hill was extra steep and the brakes on the heavy band wagon failed. As the wagon gained momentum, the lead team of the six-horse hitch became frightened and started running.

Joe built a quick loop, dashed alongside and ropped it over the necks of both horses. With rope anchored to the horn, he attempted to use his pony to bring the team to a halt. The weight of a pair of heavy draft horses proved to much for a 900-pound cow horse. The pony fell to the pavement, breaking Joe's leg. The rope held, however, and the weight of the pony was enough to slow the runaways until the other *vaqueros,* racing up from behind, brought the team under control as the wagon swerved toward the curb. Without Joe's quick thinking and rope, many spectators who lined the route might have been injured or killed.

They took Joe to the hospital. A few days later, his leg in a cast, he returned to the show, needing assistance only in mounting.

He was hero again at Chicago. The show's champion lady bronc rider, Lulu Parr, was badly injured and knocked senseless when thrown by an outlaw. She would have been dragged to death but for the timely intervention of Joe's lasso.

While Miss Parr was recovering, Joe tried to ride the wild ones. At Ypsilante, Michigan, he tackled Dynamite, a bay bucker. One of the handlers hitched the halter rope beneath the animal's forelegs in order for Joe to mount. As they started off, the rope tangled, throwing both horse and rider. Joe landed in the reserved section, lacerated severely about the arms and head.

He suffered additional injuries at Battle Creek, when he made a jump for a bucker that refused to let him mount.

Two weeks later, at Coldwater, another bronc he had mounted went through the horse tent, taking the canvas with him. The only casualty was a spectator under the influence, who injured himself when he fell through the bleachers.

Although a great horseman, Joe became wary of this type of work. Once Pawnee Bill sent him to a nearby ranch to pick up a horse to be trained for a certain act. When the cowboy in charge pointed out the good looking bay and commented that he was a more likely prospect than the show's famed Dynamite, Joe replied, in his unique vernacular: "He no buckey, I takee; he buckey, I no wannee."

Mexican Joe was in charge of the show's "rough string" for years, but his chief responsibility was Pawnee Bill's buffaloes. His ability in this area was surpassed only by his talent for butchering the King's English. In bringing the wily animals from the train to the show grounds, his *vaqueros* were inclined to chase the calves. Joe's voice would boom out above their yells: "Damee, no runee the lilly buffalo!"

Joe put his lariat to another special use during the show seasons. An act billed as "The Fatal Drag" depicted the manner in which vigilantes dealt with horse thieves on the frontier. Twice daily, Joe and his *vaqueros* would swoop down on Frank L. Sylvis, the luckless victim, lasso him and drag him from a stolen mount. Then off around the arena sped the captors, Sylvis prostrate at the end of Joe's *maguey,* struggling vainly to free himself, and the target of continuous rounds of blank ammunition. A telegraph pole at one end of the arena was finally reached. The rope was looped over the cross-piece, and Sylvis, half-stranged and choking from dust and gunsmoke, was hauled to the top. After a few spasmodic kicks, he hung limp until cut down by a pursuing sheriff's posse.

Crowds constantly wondered how Sylvis survived the ordeals. To one unbelieving reporter's inquiry, he confided: "I fear every time I'm jerked off my feet that it may be my last hanging; but the way Joe fastens that lariat always saves me."

In the decade following 1900, Beverly, Ohio, was a favorite winter quarters for circuses. Through the winter months both the small fry and adults of the town were privileged to gaze upon the colorful steam calliopes, circus wagons and the finest stock in the nation. S.M. Humston, later Beverly's mayor, housed the baggage horses in his huge E-shaped barn, and at $6 per month per head, furnished the animals corn and roughage daily. The barn became the gathering point for local farmers, who looked with envy upon the powerful horses and trim ponies.

Added to the luster was the presence of some of the best performers in the show world. There was the great John Robinson shows, a family unit that traveled out of Cincinnati, and Eugene Patterson, the big team driver who handled a twenty-horse hitch and was billed as the "California Mountain Expert," although he confided to local friends that he was "from No'th Caroline an' ain't never seen Californey." A huge man, weighing nearly 300 pounds, Patterson entertained downtown loafers by riding a horse that would kneel to allow him to mount or dismount.

Then came the western ponies and buffalo of Pawnee Bill, in charge of the famed Mexican Joe. Joe entertained with his rope. When a buffalo bull broke out of the barn and wandered into the nearby streets, Joe's expert loop tossing soon had the people breathing easier.

It was Mexican Joe who really captured the imagination and hearts of the village, especially the heart of one of its attractive young ladies, Effie May Cole. They were married at Beverly, February 23, 1905. That spring, when the ponies and buffalo were loaded aboard the railroad cars to join the main body of the show for its annual tour, Effie went with her husband. She soon got into his rope acts and became a star performer herself.

In 1913, after the combined Pawnee Bill and Buffalo Bill shows were closed at Denver, Pawnee Bill retired to his Blue Hawk Peak ranch near Pawnee, Oklahoma, and turned his attention to the future of his state. He increased his land holdings to 2,000 acres and invested in cattle and oil. Much of his ranch was placed under cultivation to feed his various animals, but most of it was retained in its primitive wildness for his buffalo and bands of Indian ponies. Two miles west of his headquarters on U.S. Highway 64, he built Old Town and an Indian trading post, his monument to the frontier past. Its museum housed his extensive collection of Indian and pioneer relics and foreign artifacts acquired during his travels in Canada, Europe and Mexico.

Joe and Effie associated themselves with various other acts and circuses. Joe put on the first Wild West Concert for Ringling Brothers in 1914, traveled three years with the Miller Brothers' 101 Ranch show, and once led his own group of cowboys and Indians on a tour of France, Spain, Por-

99

tugal and Italy. He divided his off season periods between Blue Hawk Peak and Effie's folks in Ohio.

But the golden days of the Wild West show were waning. Finally, Joe quit the sawdust circuit for good. Here is Effie's version of how it ended:

We were traveling with an act called Young Buffalo's Wild West Show Train. I awoke one morning in Alton, Illinois, where we played the night before, to find everything quiet and nobody around. I got up, dressed and walked out onto the platform of our sleeping car, and was amazed to find that the sleeping cars were all that was left on the side track. My husband had left early, as it was his custom to look after the show stock as soon as the train got in town each morning.

At that moment a Negro porter came in sight, and I asked, "Where is everybody?" He said, "Ma'am, the show is busted." My heart sank. He also told me that the show had been sold and the stock cars and flats were five miles out at the edge of town.

Marie, a girl I chummed with, came running out of the sleeping car next to mine when she heard us talking. She asked, "What's all this about the show being busted?" I repeated what the porter had told me. She dressed hurriedly and asked the porter to direct us to the show train. He said, "Ma'am, the railroad is trying to get the show across the line into Missouri where it will be safe from the employes. There's forty Negro canvasmen and cowboys guarding it with guns."

Everything Joe and I owned was on that train. "Marie," I said, "let's go up there anyway. At least we can try to get something to eat."

When we reached the show train, the cook-house wagons had unloaded alongside the tracks and the boys had all the saddle horses and baggage stock tied alongside the stock car, feeding them. We asked about breakfast. The cook-house manager said, "Girl, we'll feed what we have — black coffee and bread."

My husband was in the baggage car looking for our trunks and saddles. All my jewelry was in my trunk, including my diamond ring. About that time a friend of ours from Alton came up. He had heard that we were stranded and wanted to know if we needed anything. Joe said, "We need money to get out of here. I must pawn Effie's ring." The friend said, "I know a fellow I think will lend you some money on it." So he and Joe left for town on the run.

Some engines were puffing in the distance, but the boys were on the alert. Already they had run off three engines that had come out to hook onto the show train. The managers of the show were hiding in the hotel, afraid they would be mobbed for doing so cowardly a thing.

Marie and I went back to the sleeping cars to wait for Joe. Some Indians were lying on the ground near the tracks. They had been drinking quite heavily. One old Indian sighted us and came staggering over, and said, "I

101

wants my money." Nobody had been paid in three weeks. I told him the show would pay off soon. "I wants it now," he insisted. He climbed the platform steps and shook his fist in my face. "If I don't get pay, I kill you." He was so drunk he thought we were the owners of the show.

I tried to tell him differently, but he kept shouting "I wants my pay now." Marie and I were so frightened we ducked inside, ran through the car and jumped off the other end. We ran down the opposite side of the cars and didn't stop until we were out of sight of the Indians. We could hear them going through the cars, cursing and yelling, "We wants our money."

We reached a little German restaurant and ran inside. When we told the woman there our troubles, she gave us a room to stay in until we could leave town.

After dark, a big van came down the street. It stopped at the corner under a light and began unloading our trunks. Some of the boys had succeeded in getting our stuff off the train. They piled everything in our room. My jewelry was still in my trunk, and I felt greatly relieved. Joe came up and explained, "The man has agreed to give us some money on your ring." I gave it to Joe, and he hurried back to town. We had no way of knowing how long we would be there or what the outcome would be.

Well, everyone was peaceable except the Indians. The sheriff finally got busy — he was afraid there would be a riot — and made the managers pay everyone a week's salary so they could leave town. The Indians were sent back to their South Dakota reservation; the rest of us got jobs with others shows, going our separate ways. Joe and I took eight of our best cowboys to Omaha and joined Ringling Brothers. We finished with a grand season and went home to Ohio.

The Berraras had a young daughter, Mary Louise, to look after now, and following the uncertain show business was hardly a way to rear a child. Joe wrote Pawnee Bill. Lillie offered him a permanent position as his ranch foreman, and Joe moved his family to Blue Hawk Peak.

Mexican Joe managed Blue Hawk Peak Ranch, and little Mary became Pawnee Bill's secretary. Mrs. Lillie was killed in an automobile accident in 1936, and in 1942, Pawnee Bill died as the result of injuries received in the same crash.

In 1945, Joe lost Effie.

He moved into a house on the ranch that Pawnee Bill had given Mary and made his home with his daughter, who was now married. He continued to take care of the buffalo herds and Indian ponies for the Lillie heirs.

His last performance was at the annual Pawnee Bill Memorial Rodeo at Blue Hawk Peak on July 4, 1949. In declining health and afoot (he hadn't ridden a horse in two years), he roped four horses racing abreast.

A few weeks later he entered the Pawnee hospital for an operation. The attendant complications were too much for his 73 years. On November 16, the colorful old trooper rode off into the Great Adventure.

JOSE BARRERA and wife, Effie. Effie, a Beverly, Ohio girl, got into Joe's rope act and became a star performer.

JOSE BARRERA (on rearing horse).

JOSE BARRERA (fourth from left) with his *vaqueros* **in front of show tent.**

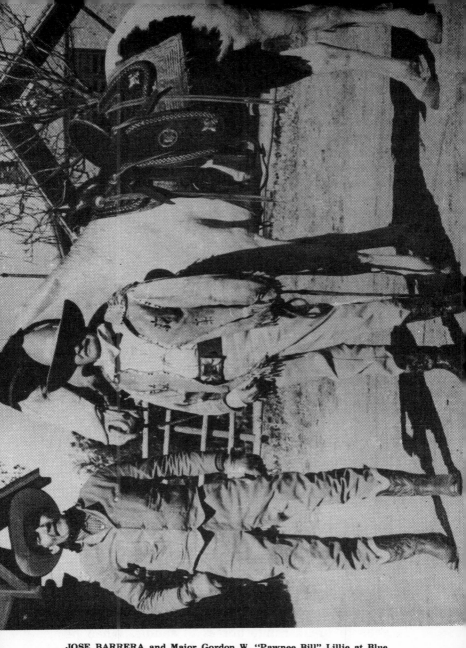

JOSE BARRERA and Major Gordon W. "Pawnee Bill" Lillie at Blue Hawk Peak Ranch after Joe became Lillie's foreman.

6. Pint-Sized Bronc Twister

Little banty-legged Billy McGinty was one red West cowboy who proved you couldn't judge a man's grit by his size. At age fourteen, he stood five-feet-four, never grew taller, and never weighed over 130 pounds. For the next thirty years he broke horses on ranches in Oklahoma, Texas, Arizona and New Mexico. During one winter in the Big Bend country northeast of El Paso, he "rode out" 413 broncs that he "kept count of." There is no doubt that Billy straddled as much leather as any man on the frontier.

"Maybe," he once quipped, "it was because horses figured they didn't have to buck very hard to throw me."

He was born in Mercer County, Missouri, January 1, 1871, the son of Robert and Margaret Ann (Burrell) McGinty. His father was a deputy sheriff and operated a stock farm near Princeton. Billy's mother died when he was six, and the family moved to Cowley County, Kansas, east of Winfield. Later, they moved to a claim in Clarke County. Dodge City was still a big shipping point on the western cattle trails, but the country was filling up with homesteaders. Robert McGinty broke the prairie sod and bottom land with a team of oxen.

Billy thought he was old enough to go off on his own. He already had decided he wasn't "cut out to bust sod." He got a job on the old Mack Mann ranch southwest of Dodge.

Bronc-busting wasn't a business a young man would choose naturally. It was dangerous work in which most men didn't last ten years. Billy "sort of drifted into it."

He started as a cowboy. But part of his work was to break range horses to saddle. When he had learned to stick on a bucker pretty well, Mann gave him harder ones to try.

During this period he formed most of his riding habits. "Many of the boys depended on brute strength to hold themselves tight in the saddle," Billy said. "Mann himself was a power rider. But I rode by feel and balance. It was just like dancing — you got in step with your partner."

The rest came from lots of practice and hundreds of hours in the saddle on all kinds of horses. Within a few years Billy became known as a horse-breaker and rough string man throughout the Southwest.

A horse-breaker was hired by a cow outfit to take the edges off a colt, train him to neck rein, to stop and start as his rider indicated, to cut a single cow from a herd, to breast and outdodge a steer and do his part at the end of a rope. In short, Billy explained,

> you got rid of a colt's fear of the man on his back and taught him to do whatever his rider wanted. To do this, you had to win the colt's full respect and be able to ride anything you throwed your saddle on.
>
> Bucking was natural for most horses. Besides high spirits, the main reason for bucking was to get rid of the rider. When I turned over a colt as broke, he was supposed to make a good cow horse. A good cowboy knew how to control him and appreciated his vigor when, now and then, he put on a little act. If the cowboy let him think he was stronger than his rider, the horse became "spoiled" and ended up in the rough string. Once he had throwed his rider a few times, he never failed to try his tricks on anybody. If handled too rough, he fought back. Often he turned outlaw and bucked all his life.

Horses in the rough string were too risky for range work. Other horses had to be handled, calves roped, castrated and branded. Spooky cows had to be trailed through mean country in all kinds of weather. At a ticklish moment on a slippery trail, or when the rope end héld a fighting steer, a rough horse might "break in tow" when his rider's attention was divided and result in the cowboy being thrown and trampled or dragged to death.

These things Billy learned the hard way as he drifted from one outfit to another, rounding up a bunch of spayed wild heifers for the Comanche Pool in the gypsum bluff country of Barber County, Kansas, then working for the Bar X Bar down in the Cherokeé Outlet, in the Pawnee "Triangle" country formed by the confluence of the Arkansas and Cimarron rivers.

The Outlet was leased by large cattle companies. Some of the owners resided as far away as Canada and London. These companies fenced vast pastures, according to the number of cattle each member, or pool of members, wished to graze. The Bar X Bar, one of the largest, handled a great portion of the Texas herds.

The herds were unloaded at Red Fork station, a spur on the Frisco railroad building southwest from Tulsa. Here Billy worked with the slow, gander-eyed, sandy-moustached Bill Doolin and two other young cowboys, Charley Pierce and Bitter Creek Newcomb, from the Turkey Track range south of the Cimarron in the Creek Nation.

Billy recalled that

> Doolin was a silent cuss who grinned little, but was a real comedian once he got started. He would wrap his big hand almost twice around the butt of a six-shooter and empty it at a target

without missing a shot. Pierce and Newcomb had wild streaks in them. Tulsa was an Indian settlement. They would ride up there and shoot out the lights just for fun. Pretty soon they were riding with the Dalton boys, robbing banks and trains.

The Daltons met disaster at Coffeyville. Doolin, Pierce and Newcomb became the nucleus of a new outlaw band that terrorized Indian Territory and the border states for years before they were killed by citizen posses and United States marshals. Billy remembered them as "just cowboys."

When the Unassigned Lands (Old Oklahoma) were opened to white settlers April 22, 1889, Billy left the Bar X Bar "to make the run." He was too young to take a claim, but he knew the country and helped his father find a good quarter section southeast of Ingalls. He stayed around a couple of months, helping him "prove up," then took a job with the A66, a Texas outfit with a summer pasture in the Outlet. That fall, the A66 shipped its herd from Pond Creek and sent Billy to its Texas ranch near Pecos City.

The next three years Billy worked on roundups and in cow camps from the Pecos to the Rio Grande, and trailed one herd of "mean, stampeding longhorns" to a steer ranch between the Big and Little Missouri rivers in Dakota.

He was "sure glad" to reach the end of the drive. He stayed just long enough to see those "no'thern lights" cowboys talked about before returning to Texas.

Trail work didn't appeal to him, and he went back to breaking horses.

Bustin' broncs was easy after having to worry about roundups, trail herds

111

and stampedes. I could lay down and
sleep nights, and got more money.

He hired out to Joe Nations at El Paso. Nations owned two ranches — the Seven Half-H on the plains to the north, and the Star, about ten miles southeast of old Fort Hancock. He put Billy to work on the Star.

The trail driving business since the Civil War had scattered the Spanish pony from the Rio Grande to Canada. As the demand for Spanish horses increased, northern cattlemen sent men who were good judges of horseflesh to buy them for breeding stock. The animals could be bought at $5 to $7 a head in Mexico, or rounded up on the plains from wild herds, and sold at $25 to $35. Primarily a cattleman, Nations made much of his ranch expenses breeding, breaking and training herds of broncs. Like others in the business, he preferred to contract the breaking end to reliable riders at so much a head.

Usually two busters were put in camp to help each other. They weren't expected to break more than a dozen broncs a month. They would run a bronc into a round corral, rope his forefeet, throw him on the ground and put on a hackamore with about thirty feet of rope, then let him get up and lead him around to gentle him some. Next, they would slap him on the back and hips with a blanket until he quit flinching, then throw on the saddle and drag it off a few times before it was finally cinched up. If the bronc still spooked, he was allowed to buck around the corral at rope's end until he quit. Then he was fed and watered. The bronc then would be ridden in the corral a couple of times, and finally ridden outside, accompanied by the second rider on a gentle horse. After four or five saddles, the bronc was taken out and galloped and turned and made used to man and rope. If he didn' pan out, he was re-

112

turned to the corral for "more education."

Billy worked differently than most busters. He

had no helper. I would get up early,
ride my stake pony up the mountain
and corral a bunch of broncs about
four miles from camp. I'd rope one,
snub him to a post, then put my hackamore and saddle on him and ride him
in the corral. Then I'd turn loose my
stake pony and follow him back to
camp on the bronc.

At camp, I'd put the bronc on a stake
rope and hobble him, and next time
ride another bronc back. Then I'd ride
the bronc I'd staked out first, and repeat the routine until I had eight
broncs on the rope. Then I'd ride all
eight the same day.

When I had them broke to hackamore, hobble and bridle, I'd turn them
over to the ranch cowboys to finish off.
Some were sold to neighboring ranches. Most of them went to Kansas or
Beaver City, in No Man's Land.

Billy delivered his last herd of horses for Joe
Nations the summer of 1893, in Iowa. He

wired Nations his money, then went to
Ingalls, Oklahoma, to visit my father.
The Cherokee Outlet was about to be
opened to homesteaders and the whole
country was excited. Father was pros-
pering on the farm he'd got in '89, and
I decided to make the run into the Outlet and get a quarter section for myself.

I had a place in mind in the Pawnee
"Triangle" where I'd worked on the

Bar X Bar. The morning of September 16, I rode to the nearest entry point northeast of Ingalls. I found men, women and even children there in every kind of vehicle, muleback, horseback and afoot. The soldiers had a time holding them back, and when the bugles blew and their carbines cracked at noon, nothing could have stopped them. I never saw such a horse race!

As in the '89 opening, there was trouble with "sooners" — people who slipped in before time, hid in the brush along the creeks, then joined the race at different points with fresh teams and saddle horses. Some were arrested by the soldiers. Some disputes were settled with rifles and six-shooters.

I'd just staked my quarter section when I found it was occupied by another fellow who swore he was there first. I knew he was a sooner, but couldn't prove it. I had my saddle gun handy, but decided to ride to the land office at Perry and file my claim before the other fellow got there.

At Perry, people were standing in front of the land office in two lines half a mile long. I got in line and waited, sleeping and eating there three days and nights, only to learn that the other fellow had beat me by filing by mail.

I wasn't happy about it. I could have contested him. But contests were long-drawn-out affairs, and the party who filed first usually got the best of it.

Billy drifted east to Pawnee. The town was booming, and he opened a livery business and camp yard.

114

A fellow came through with a good herd of horses. I traded him my livery business and put the herd on winter pasture near Ripley, on the Cimarron.

Oklahoma was "settling up" and range land becoming scarce. In the spring, Billy sold his horses at a good profit and went to New Mexico. He broke broncs for ranches around El Capitan Mountain and Lordsburg, then moved on to Arizona. It was round-up time and Bob Casey, who owned the CA Bar on the Gila below Duncan, the little town that had withstood so many sieges by the warring tribes of Geronimo, was looking for a buster.

Billy remembered that

the ranch kept its horses on Rattlesnake Mountain. They had to be broken and shod, and Casey sent me up the mountain to report to a strawboss named Johnson.

I was a little late arriving, and it made Johnson mighty ringy. He went down to headquarters and asked Casey, "Where'd you get that Mormon kid?" I learned later he'd had trouble once in Utah and called everyone he didn't cotton to a Mormon.

He tried to deal me misery right off by seeing that I was assigned a certain gray horse. Casey was a nice fellow and would never have let Johnson pull the trick if I hadn't told him horses never jumped too high for me. The gray had throwed one cowboy and trampled him to death. Even if I'd known that, it wouldn't have made a difference. I liked to rake the wild ones around.

The moment I hit the saddle the fun

115

began. That was about the meanest bronc I ever tackled. It was tough going for several minutes, but when I got off that gray, he knew he'd been rode. The boys gave Johnson the laugh, and he'd take out every time they'd ask about "that Mormon kid."

During roundup, a horse fell on Johnson and busted his leg. It was miles to a doctor. I set the leg, disinfected it with boiling water and made a splint from a mesquite limb. While he was laid up in camp, I carried his meals, and "that Mormon kid" was never mentioned again.

The roundup was on the west side of the range called Buzzards Roost. The country was so rough the chuck wagons had to be held along the river. It was all mesa and mountains and the cattle were as wild and agile as mountain sheep. When we run them down the trails they got so mad and hot we had to rope and tie them down to cool them off.

The roundup over, Billy went to the tough mining town of Clifton. Jim Parks was deputy sheriff for the area, "a very dangerous position." But Parks was a fearless lawman and proved more than a match for the rough element. He appointed Billy special officer to collect taxes from the gamblers. Billy also "helped him capture the Bell brothers and trail the Apache Kid."

It wasn't Billy's type of work, however. He resigned to start ranching on his own, and bought half interest in the 80 brand.

This was another mountain outfit, with cattle even wilder and harder to

handle. Calves followed their mothers
longer in the mountains, often sucking
until ten months old. They stayed in
the high country during the snows,
didn't have to travel far to water and
got fatter in the winter than summer.
So there was little loss on this range . .

Despite his mountain experience on the CA
Bar, Billy had new things to learn. The south-
east range was claimed by the Morenci Copper
Company, using the Terrapin brand. The south-
west part was owned by a man named Tuck
Dale. Up the Frisco river, over the mountains,
was a horse ranch owned by a half-breed called
Indian Charley.

I bought my saddle stock from Charley. The first time I tried branding
calves I found these horses weren't fast
enough to catch them. I tried turning
them up the mountains, but still
couldn't get a rope near them. Then I
discovered all the horses were "coon-
footed."
Charley's saddle stock were bred to
mountain mares — mares that were
dropped down at the ankles and run as
much on the ankle as on the hoof. Coon
feet were caused by young colts climb-
ing the trails after their mothers. In-
breeding produced more coon-footed
colts. Such horses were worthless in
rough country. But I'd got them at a
bargain and had no kick coming.

Billy stayed on the 80 range two years, then
sold to Tuck Dale. The United States had declared war on Spain, and he hurried back to
Oklahoma to join Roosevelt's Rough Riders,

"made up of eight men from each county in Arizona, New Mexico, Texas and the Oklahoma and Indian territories." Billy was one of the first of some 230 men from the Twin Territories to pass examination at Guthrie.

He was assigned to Troop D at San Antonio. Then Roosevelt and Colonel Leonard Wood arrived and "changed things around," and he was transferred to Troop K.

Troop K consisted mostly of "rich men's sons from the East — hunters and polo players." Many had been all over the world and had joined the Rough Riders to find new adventure. But Billy found them to be "fine fellows, willing to do their part anytime, anywhere." He especially liked his captain, Woodbury Kane, who had been "one of Teddy's close friends at Harvard."

Once organized, the troop began receiving horses. Most were South Texas and Mexican mustangs, hard to handle on picket lines and to feed and water. Nearly all had to be broken. Billy and four other bronc riders were assigned the task.

Next they were told that Cuba was very mountainous country and the horses would have to be shod at once. Billy wasn't detailed for this work, but he had shod plenty of horses for mountain work in Arizona and remarked to Captain Kane that the troopers were very slow in handling them. "If the boys would tie them down, they could do it faster and easier."

Billy roped a horse by the forefeet and threw him to the ground. Then he tied him above the hocks and front knees with legs crossed and sticking in the air and placed a log on each side to keep him from rolling. Then all four shoes were put on at once.

They were working near Roosevelt's tent, and finally the colonel came over. Billy thought he was

118

in for a bawling out. But Roosevelt knew the West. After watching me shoe the horse, he exclaimed: "That was bully!" It was a common expression with him when pleased, and the beginning of our friendship which lasted through his years in the White House.

Billy measured up with the tallest, toughest troopers in everything except drill. A lieutenant rebuked him for lagging on a foot march.

"I'm too small to keep up with the others, sir," Billy replied. "But if you will give me a horse, I'll keep up with the best of them."

Roosevelt affectionately granted his preference in transportation, and afterwards said of him: "He would never walk a hundred yards if by any chance he could ride."

But in the Cuban campaign, the hard-riding little cavalryman and his comrades became Teddy's Weary Walkers. Half the regiment was left in Tampa, Florida, because of a shortage of boats. Billy's troop went over on a cattle boat, bedded down in straw.

They met the Spaniards at Las Guasimas, June 24, 1898, then at El Poso and El Caney, and on July 1, smashed their fortifications in the charge up San Juan Hill and dug in for the siege of Santiago.

The next morning they found that about fifty men had overrun the hill and were cut off from the main forces 200 yards away in direct line of Spanish guns. Using small daggers, they were digging back and taking cover in shallow trenches along the hillside. It would be impossible to rescue them before nightfall. The sun beat down.

"They can't stay in that sun all day without food and drink," Roosevelt said.

"I'll take them something," volunteered Billy.

"I'll go with you," Roosevelt said.

119

Captain Kane objected. "No, Colonel. The regiment is depending on you, but no one is depending on us. I'll go."

Billy told Captain Kane: "No sense risking two men. I'll take them a case of tomatoes."

Kane finally consented.

Billy shouldered the canned tomatoes, ducked low and dashed for the outpost. When he hit the brow of the hill, he thought the whole Spanish army had opened fire on him.

He kept close to the ground and his size helped. Lead ripped into the case on his back. But he reached his buddies with nothing more than tomato juice running down his face and neck. He found a hole and crawled in, then started digging back with the others until the main trenches were reached.

The army cited Billy for bravery in action. Later, the Cuban government awarded him a certificate and medal in recognition of the role he had played as a Rough Rider. He served as an aide to Roosevelt after the Rough Riders reached New York.

While the troops were being discharged at Montauk Point, the colonel asked him to take his favorite horse, Little Tex, to his home at Oyster Bay. All along the route souvenir hunters beset Billy, pulling hairs from the tail of the mount of the hero of San Juan.

When Roosevelt saw the horse, he remarked: "Bully! but he surely looks funny."

Billy never told him what happened.

After his discharge, Billy joined a show in New York called The Battle of All Nations, in which he played the role of General Joe Wheeler, the hero of Santiago. He remained in New York until Roosevelt was elected governor. Roosevelt offered him a job in the park service, but Billy wanted to get back to Oklahoma. During the 1893 visit with his father, he had met Mollie

Pickering, an Ingalls girl. They had corresponded regularly. At Ingalls, he found a letter waiting for him from Johnny Baker, a director of Buffalo Bill's Wild West show, and for the next two years he toured the country with Cody, riding broncs and playing the role of General Wheeler in a miniature reproduction of The Battle of San Juan Hill and his famous presentation Three Minutes With the Rough Riders of the World.

Show business, however, wasn't something Billy wanted to follow the rest of his life. At the close of the 1901 season, he returned to Oklahoma, married Mollie and started his Crossed Sabers ranch in old Day County, on the border of the Texas panhandle. He found ranching not as profitable as before, but "stayed in Day County until the sand storms and homesteaders ran him out," then moved to Ingalls, finally settling at Ripley, to rear his family of three children.

In 1907, he went east again, traveling with the Frederic Remington Act sponsored by the famed Montana bronc rider, Kid Gabriel. In this act, Billy rode a bucking horse on a stage.

"I was the first man ever to do that," Billy claimed. "The performance took place in the old Vanderbilt Theater in New York City, the year Oklahoma became a state."

He went east again in 1910, when Roosevelt called in his friends for the meeting at Sagamore Hill and the Bull Moose Party was organized. At this meeting, some of the boys suggested that the world bronc-riding championship should go to a Rough Rider. Roosevelt asked: "How about McGinty?" And on July 4, Billy took the championship from Bert Bryan, the Arizona cowboy, in a riding duel at Southampton, Long Island.

Back in Oklahoma, Billy held various positions under state officials who had been Rough Riders. Show business still drew him. When the first radio station went on the air in 1924, he headed up a group of musicians dedicated to acquainting a new generation with the old songs of the range and trail.

> We started as an all-string unit for local programs and dances. Our popularity soon brought us into the studios in the east. I had sort of a national reputation as a showman and fronted for the organization. We called it "McGinty's Oklahoma Cowboy Band."

And they looked the part — lean, bronzed, with their two-gallon Stetsons, high-healed boots and leather batwing and Angora chaps. They were the first band to put cowboy songs on phonograph records. By 1930, they were being heard over 130 radio stations and were a regular feature on the Red and Blue Network of NBC.

Billy left the organization that year to become postmaster at Ripley, a position he held until he retired in 1949. He "kept busy" attending old settlers reunions, frontier celebrations and meetings of the National Rough Riders Association. For a decade he served as its vice-president. In 1954, he was elected president for life.

Only a handful of the nearly 600 veterans of that colorful, hell-for-leather outfit were able to make the 1960 gathering at Las Vegas, New Mexico. Billy had to be boosted onto his horse for the parade. He didn't have trouble staying on. For him, riding came natural.

"He rode every bronc that came down the pike," boasted a cowboy friend, and described how Billy had ridden one unbroken horse. "He slipped the saddle, discarding it, then the bridle, and continued riding the frantic animal successfully."

"I would never tell that one," Billy objected. "Most folks wouldn't believe it."

But a few days before his death on May 21, 1961, at age 90, he admitted: "What my friend said is true — I've never been throwed by a bronc, including the 413 I broke that winter on the Star near El Paso."

BILLY McGINTY breaking a "wild one" for the Rough Riders at San Antonio, 1898.

BILLY McGINTY, pint-sized bronc twister, in typical pose.

BILLY ESPECIALLY LIKED his Rough Rider captain, Woodbury Kane, one of Roosevelt's "close friends" at Harvard.

COLONEL THEODORE ROOSEVELT was impressed by Billy's horse-shoeing methods, the beginning of a friendship which lasted through his years in the White House.

126

TROOP K, Rough Riders, at San Antonio, Texas, 1898.

THE CHARGE AT San Juan Hill (from painting by Frederic Remington).
The army cited Billy for bravery in action, and the Cuban government
awarded him a certificate and medal in recognition of the role he played
as a Rough Rider.

128

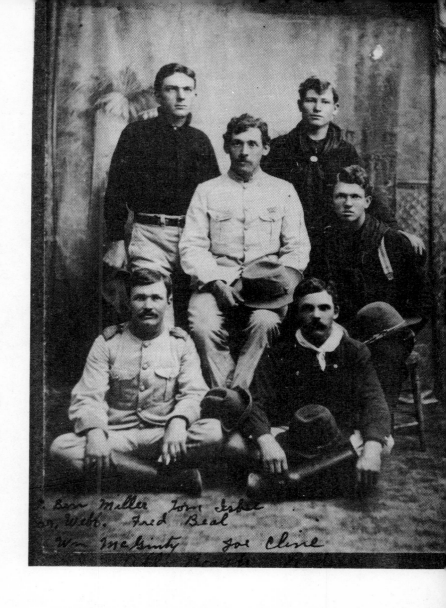

BILLY McGINTY and Rough Rider friends in New York after discharge at Montauk Point. (L to R, back row: Ben Miller, Tom Isbell; center: Sergeant Webb, Fred Beal; on floor, front: McGinty and Joe Cline.)

BILLY McGINTY with the Frederic Remington Act in New York City, 1907, where he became the first man to ride a bucking bronc on a theater stage.

BILLY McGINTY (left) and the famed Western artist Ed Borein at South-
hampton, Long Island, in July, 1910 when Billy took the world bronc-
riding championship from Bert Bryan, Arizona cowboy.

BOOK 3

"The sensation of the day was created by 'The California Girl' whose forte is shooting at a swinging target. She complicates her feat by adding all kinds of difficulties to her aim, and her crowning achievements of smashing a glass ball made to revolve horizontally at great speed, and clearing off ball after ball on the target just mentioned to the number of *twenty*, were really marvelous."

—London *Times*

7. Princess Wenona

Debunking has become something of an American pastime. Skeptics have maintained that the George Washington hatchet and cherry tree incident is just another myth, and other historic figures down the centuries have been stripped of glamor until they look like ordinary folk. This tradition has included many characters of the American West.

Legends, false or not, add to a nation's glories and make our lives richer by their telling. Without these stories students of history might not do their homework and hundreds who helped shape our frontier might have died in anonymity. A case in point is Lillian Smith, female sharpshooter in the sawdust ring for thirty-five years, known as "The California Girl" and "Princess Wenona."

Like many comparatively unknowns in real life, she gained her fame in the Wild West shows of the 1880s and 1890s. Pasts often were confused by the manufactured publicity so characteristic of show build-ups given star performers. At almost every stand press agents and brochure writers seemed to rush back to their dictionaries to hunt new adjectives to describe this one and that one's prowess, and the performers themselves seemed not unwilling, from time to time, to have their biographies rewritten. Lillian Smith was no exception.

She joined the Buffalo Bill Wild West troupe in Los Angeles in 1885. William F. Cody allegedly visited a local shooting gallery and was "so amazed at this young girl of fifteen, who made his own efforts seem like the attempts of a novice," that he signed her immediately.

She made her first appearance at the St. Louis Fair Grounds the spring of 1886. Annie Oakley — "Little Sure Shot," conferred on her by the famous Sioux leader Sitting Bull — had joined the show the year previous. Johnny Baker, striding in Cody's shadow, his hair inching down over his shirt collar, but not old enough to grow a mustache and goatee, was her closest competitor as "The Cowboy Kid." Buffalo Bill biographers claim it was Annie's popularity that convinced Cody and his partner, Nate Salsbury, they should add three other women performers — Della Farrell and Georgia Duffy, cowgirls from Colorado and Wyoming, who staged daily pony races, and Lillian Smith, "the California huntress."

The publicity stated that

> Lil was born in Coleville, Mono County, California. Tired of playing with dolls at age seven, she took up the rifle, shooting forty mallards and redheads a day on the wing and bobcats out of the towering redwoods.

Buffalo Bill's Wild West, for the first time, carried its own seats with a canvas canopy, lighting system, and huge wood and canvas background of colored buttes and mountains. The company consisted of nearly 250 canvasmen, teamsters, roustabouts and new performers. Sitting Bull had left the show to be replaced by two Sioux chiefs, American Horse and Rocky Bear. American Horse headed the Indians. Sergeant Bates, the exhibitionist Civil War veteran who had traveled from coast to coast carrying a large American flag and giving patriotic lectures, was a feature. Among the bronc busters were "Coyote Bill" Bullock, Jim Kidd on White Emigrant, the bucker on which he had won the Montana championship in 1884, and "Sunday Jim" Mitchell, "Cowboy Preacher of the Plains," on his famous bucking black mare Dynamite. Buck

Taylor was "King of the Cowboys," Billy Johnson was Pony Express rider, and Antonio Esquivel leader of the *vaqueros*. "Custer's Massacre climaxed the program with noise, color and drama still fresh on the pages of history.

Lil was billed as interlude entertainment to hold the attention of the crowd while the big acts were being changed. She would hit a plate thirty times in fifteen seconds, then break ten glass balls hung from strings and swinging around a pole. When ball after ball had been shattered, she would destroy the strings without a miss. In the final part of this act she would toss a ball into the air, then fire at it three times and miss — purposely. She always shattered it on the fourth shot.

Without railroad equipment at that time, a series of one-day stands was not possible and Cody was forced to play long engagements in large cities. The show stayed six months during the summer at a resort operated by Erastus Wiman on Staten Island, New York. Here Lil won a place of her own on the program. Her audience demanded it. She broke 495 out of 500 balls with a Ballard .22, and was viewed from the stands by such notables as General W.T. Sherman, Mark Twain, P.T. Barnum, Thomas A. Edison and Elizabeth Custer. During one week in July nearly 200,000 applauding spectators were "brought screaming to their feet with her amazing ability."

Since he had found her in Los Angeles, Cody called her "The California Girl." The story now released stated she was the daughter of a lighthouse keeper somewhere on the Delaware coast. When she was seven, her father had presented her with a rifle to cope with the boredom a lighthouse keeper's daughter is supposed to endure. Lil was delighted. She would sit in a small boat and shoot ducks on the wing to perfect her marksmanship, until her father complained he was tired of duck. To vary the menu, her father entered her in a series of turkey shoots. That "provided pleasant diversions in both diet and experience" until she was expelled by the managers "to give the boys an opportunity."

The story continued:

> At age eleven, she had become so proficient at hitting most any target that her father decided she had a future. He gave up his lighthouse job and moved to Los Angeles, opening a shooting gallery with the girl as a featured attraction . . . .

Apparently the decision was a wise one. Lil had "become a legend on the West coast" when Cody discovered her.

The Erastina engagement was so successful that Cody and Salsbury decided to try for the big time and leased Madison Square Garden from Adam Forepaugh for a winter exhibition. James Morrison Steele MacKaye—manager of Madison Square Theater (1879), designed by him, who built Lyceum Theater, established the first dramatic school in America, and was himself producer and author of more than twenty plays — wrote the scenario for this Buffalo Bill pageant, called *The Drama of Civilization*. Nelse Waldron, who invented the first double (moving) stage for theater use, was in charge of the mechanical operations. MacKaye insisted on something more than the traditional stage effects, and Waldron came up with plans so vast it was necessary to raise the roof of the Garden twenty-five feet to take care of the equipment.

For instance, in one scene the city of Deadwood in the Black Hills was to be destroyed by a cyclone. Waldron had rigged up a steam-driven

ventilator system with three fans, five feet in dia-
meter, to keep fresh air moving through the
building. The cyclone came off perfectly. One
hundred bags of dried leaves, opened in front of
the fans, were whipped across the stage "quite
realistically."

At Erastina, Mark Twain had commented that

> down to its smallest details, the show
> is genuine . . . the effects it produced
> upon me by its spectacles were identi-
> cal with those wrought upon me a long
> time ago by the same spectacles on the
> frontier . . . . It is often said on the
> other side of the water that none of the
> exhibitions which we send to England
> are purely and distinctive American. If
> you will take the Wild West show over
> there you can remove that reproach.

Twain referred to Queen Victoria's Golden
Jubilee (celebrating the fiftieth year of her reign)
scheduled for 1887 in London. American promot-
ers had organized "An Exhibition of the Arts, In-
dustries, Manufactures, Products and Resources
of the United States." They took note of Twain's
suggestion and offered Cody and Salsbury their
facilities and a percentage of the gate receipts to
include Buffalo Bill's Wild West on the program.
The partners, long anxious to show in Europe,
accepted.

The show arrived at Gravesend on the State
Line steamship *State of Nebraska* April 16, was
transferred to three trains and taken to Earl's
Court, where camp was established. On May 5,
four days before its London opening, a special
performance was given for Albert Edward,
Prince of Wales, and his royal party.

Queen Victoria was impressed by the glowing
accounts that filtered into the palace and decid-

to see for herself. A command performance, good for public relations but not for the box office, was arranged. The Queen planned to see only part of the show, but stayed for the entire entertainment.

William Sweeney's Cowboy Band of thirty-six mounted musicians gave a half-hour concert. Emma Lake, daughter of Agnes Lake, the circus owner who had married Wild Bill Hickok before his demise at Deadwood, "square-danced" on her horse that she had taught to jump, walk on his hind legs and bow to music. Custer died at the Little Big Horn, there was an attack on a settler's cabin, a buffalo hunt, and a run of the Deadwood stagecoach and the Pony Express. Buck Taylor and his cowboys and Antonio Esquivel and his *vaqueros* did trick and fancy riding and roping. Jim Kidd, who had married Lillian Smith in New York, and Jim Mitchell rode their famed buckers. The cowgirls raced their ponies, Annie Oakley and Johnny Baker did their shooting acts, and "The California Girl" broke glass balls all over the place.

At the close of the show, the Queen asked that "The California Girl" be presented. Lil pranced her horse up to the royal box, doffed her broad-brimmed sombrero and the horse courtsied. This was only the beginning. The Queen asked the girl to come into her box.

No protocol had been established for such an unexpected invitation, but Lil was up to the occasion. She took her loaded rifle into the box, for the Queen had expressed special interest in the weapon.

"Young California spoke up gracefully, and like a little lady," Cody said, telling about it later. "She showed the Queen the mechanism of the firearm, unloaded and stripped it in order that each part might be examined, then handed it to the gracious sovereign . . . all the time conversing with her Majesty as if she had been a member of the troupe."

The British press made much of the incident and described Lil's act in characteristic confusing language as follows:

> The sensation of the day was created by "The California Girl" whose forte is shooting at a swinging target. She complicates her feat by adding all kinds of difficulties to her aim, and her crowning achievements of smashing a glass ball made to revolve horizontally at great speed, and clearing off ball after ball on the target just mentioned to the number of *twenty,* were really marvelous.

The Wild West played London from May 9 to October 31. *The Times* declared it "the greatest, most unapproachable and thoroughly howling success" that America ever sent to England and called Cody "the hero of the season."

The show went to Birmingham November 5. A Manchester engagement, which ran from December 17 to April 30, was an indoor performance called *A Depiction of American History,* modeled after the Madison Square Garden pageant of the previous winter, complete with the landing of the Pilgrims at Plymouth Rock and the daring deeds of Captain John Smith. The press detailed each episode, and never failed to save space for "The California Girl":

> A brilliant display of shooting on foot and on horseback was given in the arena, and the magical promptitude with which glass balls and other small objects are shattered before her never-erring aim while riding at full speed must be seen to be believed . . . .

141

The last performance was at Hull on May 5, where crowds poured in on numerous excursion trains. Next day the show sailed for America. Upon arrival in New York, it opened another summer engagement at Erastina.

Lil met with as much popularity back in the States as she had enjoyed in Europe. In 1890, Cody posted a purse of $10,000 to anyone who could defeat her in public exhibition shooting. As far as records reveal the next fifteen years, no one ever tried — not even Annie Oakley.

When Cody and Pawnee Bill combined their shows in 1909, Lil became "Princess Wenona." They not only changed her name, but her origin.

Lil was the daughter of Crazy Horse, the famed Sioux chief, and his white wife. She was three years old when Crazy Horse was killed September 5, 1877, but she remembered that he had named her Wenona. The mother had taken her to California "to give her a proper education," but had married again, and Wenona had to do some thinking on her own.

Her preoccupation with firearms caused her to frequent the shooting galleries in Los Angeles. As her proficiency increased, she was sought after by gallery operators willing to risk a little capital "when bragging gunmen showed up to parade their skills." Wenona outshot them all. When it became difficult to find anyone foolish enough to challenge her, she joined the Wild West shows.

This story, Lil insisted, was true. In any event, it was the one she liked best. "Princess Wenona" sounded more romantic than "The California Girl." She no longer wore simple western dress as in her earlier appearances with Cody but an Indian costume, highly decorated with beads and jewelry befitting her regal title.

The Princess needed some artificial glamor. She had arrived at that stage of life when weight becomes a factor; she could still shoot with the best of them, but it was possible to see all the way across the arena that she had outgrown her dainty shape.

When Cody and Gordon Lillie closed their "Two Bills" show at Denver in 1913, the Princess and Jim Kidd (they had long been divorced) opened a small show of their own. It was a short-lived venture. However, willing hands seemed ever ready to rescue her. When the Miller brothers of Oklahoma put their 101 Ranch Wild West show back on the road after World War I, Wenona went with them.

She was still gaining weight, but still able to break glass balls. Her problem was with other glasses. Strong drink was taking its toll, and she had difficulty holding husbands. For a brief period she was married to California Frank, an old Buffalo Bill performer; then Wayne Beasley, a 101 cowboy; Eagle Shirt, a Sioux Indian with the show, and eventually the wild animal painter, Emil William Lenders.

Hard times had descended not only upon the Princess but the whole Wild West business. Public interest in lady sharp-shooters and outdoor tent shows waned with the advent of the silent screen, and "talkies" were in the offing when Colonel Joe Miller died in his garage from carbon monoxide poisoning in 1927 and George Miller met death in 1929 when his car skidded on an icy curve near Ponca City. The stock market crash that same year sucked Zack Miller under, and he limped about the country with the remains of the show he was neither able to finance or manage. The depression also spelled doom for the ranching empire. Many of the 101's top performers had become motion picture stars, but for those like the Princess, driven from the arena by years and with no place to turn, it was the end of the road.

Fortunately, the Millers had their own social security system. They maintained a neat row of cabins along the bank of the Salt Fork which once housed summer tourists who came from all parts of the world to look at the Old West. The cabins now housed a colony of old-timers, who were offered light work on the ranch if they wanted it. In one of these small buildings on the river Wenona found sanctuary.

Emil Lenders was a native of Europe, born May 11, 1864, and reared at Bingen on the Rhine. He had studied at the University of Berlin and other art institutes before coming to the United States and setting up a studio in Philadelphia. Joe Miller had met him during his first trip east with the show. Informed of Lenders' desire to study the buffalo and other animals of the plains, Joe invited him to visit the ranch. Lenders had painted farmyard scenes and domestic animals in Pennsylvania, but found something lacking. Joe told him he needed "sunlight" in his pictures.

"I found sunlight in Oklahoma," the artist said afterwards.

Lenders came to the 101 as a cowboy. Working cattle, busting broncs and living with the Indians, he learned things about western life that later made his paintings almost perfect in detail. He became a member of the five tribes in the region, learned to speak their languages, and even adopted their clothing and customs. He spent every spare moment sketching buffalo heads, snouts, legs, and painted their coats with master strokes probably better than any other artist in history.

By living with the Indians, he was able to produce likenesses of the native subjects that few painters of the American Indian have surpassed. His works also included wolves, wild horses, longhorns and domestic animals.

In 1915, at the 110th annual Philadelphia art exhibition sponsored by the Pennsylvania Academy of Fine Arts, two of his paintings were accepted. He received national and world wide attention a few years later when J.P. Morgan paid several thousand dollars for a collection of his paintings in New York. This was the only large sale of his works.

For nearly twenty years he had worked on the 101 and traveled with the show. He resided on a 20-acre tract called "Thunderbird" that he had acquired near Marland. Here Lenders kept numerous animals, including eighteen dogs, and at one time had an orchard of 500 peach trees, 500 blackberry plants and a vineyard of 5,000 grape vines. In these surroundings he produced most of his best art.

Like other 101 employees, he found times difficult. He disposed of "Thunderbird" and moved his studio into Ponca City. But he sold few paintings. He married Wenona and moved into the cabin on the Salt Fork. They raised chickens and collected dogs. At one time they had forty-eight, all strays that had wandered in and stayed. Lenders continued to paint his wild animals.

Finally he achieved fame of a sort. He was commissioned to do a number of paintings for people in Tulsa, where he moved his studio, then in Oklahoma City, where he spent the last five years of his life.

Wenona remained alone in the cabin on the 101. Almost everyone in oil-rich Ponca City knew her, but she had never been "accepted." There was talk that she was a fraud and had tricked her way through life. But she never let these things bother her. She belonged to another age, another world rich with memories, and she was content with them for companionship. She continued to care for her chickens and dogs, and in spite of the burden of years and a heavy body, made frequent visits to town to make frugal purchases, until the winter of 1930.

Weathermen still call it the coldest winter on record in Oklahoma. Snow began falling in mid-January, followed by sleet, rain and more snow. For days the temperature stood below zero. It was too much for Wenona. She died February 3.

It was a poor time for a funeral. Grave diggers complained of the frozen ground, and people were unwilling to leave warm homes to see the corpulent remains of a strange old lady laid to rest in the wind-swept cemetery.

Zack Miller was away from the ranch. W.A. "Billy" Brooks, a cousin of the Millers, was in charge, and it fell on him to arrange the funeral. He determined that Wenona should have a Christian burial. Her religious beliefs were not known, but some women in Marland who often had befriended her thought she had "deep convictions."

In searching through her personal souvenirs, Brooks found a poem, entitled "My Prayer." The author's name was missing and there was no notation why it was in Wenona's possession, but he was convinced it expressed her thinking:

God, let me live each lovely day
So I may know that come what may
I've done my best to live the way
You want me to.

Forgive me if I do not pray
The ultra-sanctimonious way
In church on every Sabbath day
As Christians do.

Just let me know if I should stray
That I may stop along the way
At any time of night or day
And talk to You.

Miss Lillian F. Smith

LILLIAN SMITH with two of her favorite weapons. For thirty-five years she was known in Wild West shows as "The California Girl" and "Princess Wenona."

GORDON W. "Pawnee Bill" Lillie and William F. "Buffalo Bill" Cody
(shown here combining their shows in 1909) not only changed Lillian
Smith's name to "Princess Wenona," but her origin. Lil became the
daughter of the famed Sioux chief, Crazy Horse.

EMIL WILLIAM LENDERS, Western artist and Princess Wenona's last husband.

Brooks persuaded a local minister to conduct the service in his church and gave him the poem as a text. After reading the poem from the pulpit, the minister declared emphatically that it did not indicate any proper Christian living and should not be accepted as such.

Brooks was dismayed, almost heartbroken. But he had succeeded in getting a church funeral and Christian burial for the old show girl. The women from Marland attended the services at both the church and grave. The pallbearers were Brooks, a local newspaperman, and four ranch cowboys, and although a dismal, blizzardly day, the clouds broke briefly and the sun shone.

8. Woman of Destiny

The faces of the 112 male delegates assembled in Convention Hall at Guthrie the afternoon of December 5, 1906, to write a constitution for the proposed state of Oklahoma, registered affection and interest as a dark-haired, bright-eyed, 27-year-old woman — so tiny that she looked like an eager child — stepped to the speaker's platform.

On either side of her sat William H. "Alfalfa Bill" Murray, president of the convention, and Vice-President Peter Hanraty, creators of the first farm-labor bloc in the West. But all eyes in the chamber were on the petite lady at the podium. They knew why she was there; the *State Capital,* Oklahoma's largest newspaper, had heralded her coming:

> Miss Kate Barnard, matron of the United Provident Association of Oklahoma City and member of the National Child Labor League, will arrive today to address the convention in the interest of three measures — child labor, compulsory education, and the creation of a department of charities . . . .

Watching her, and listening to her, with her pretty face and five feet of height, her big and blue and searching eyes and earnest young voice, it was impossible for the listeners not to think of her as a child until they remembered what she had accomplished. She looked like a school girl, talked like an idealist and she was, perhaps, a visionary; but she spoke with common sense.

> However far out on the seas of enthusiasm my eagerness might sweep me, my aim is scientific statecraft. I want to place humanity on the level of importance with finance and law, and do it by the simplest and sanest of economic methods.
> My work is a free will offering of God, and Oklahoma must, and shall, protect its children from the mill factory and awful sweat shop system!

This 96-pound bundle of nerves and human energy already had opened the eyes of old politicians by her influence and affiliations with labor. She was the constant companion of farm leaders, and those in position to know declared she controlled more votes than any man, or any party of men, in the Twin Territories.

Her recent speeches in the Chickasaw and Choctaw nations had aroused great interest in her work. Her recent talk to a party of miners 600 feet below the earth's surface at McAlester had made the child-labor question the all absorbing topic of conversation throughout the coal belt.

"She is given credit for these planks in the Democratic platform," the *Capital* added, "and it is said she will insist on their adoption as part of the constitution."

And insist, Kate Barnard did. For thirty minutes this intense, fiery little person talked with a woman's volubility, with gestures and smiles and frowns and sometimes with tears, not afraid either of showing her feelings or confessing that she had "prayed a great deal."

Her plea was so well received that her compulsory education and child labor measures were adopted at once. Her model child labor plank, passed unanimously, prohibited employment of children under the age of fifteen in occupations hazardous to health, morals, life or limb . . . .

Newspapers said her appeal was "largely personal," that she "swayed the emotions" of the delegates to make these planks a part of the constitution whether they wanted to or not; and she replied, "That is exactly what I intended to do."

And after many of her other measures had been included, the organic law accepted in Washington and the Twin Territories became a state in November, 1907, James Bryce, the noted British historian-politician and author of *The American Commonwealth* (a full exposition of the American system of government and political machinery), called Oklahoma's constitution "the finest document of human liberty since the Declaration of Independence or the Constitution of Switzerland, and no little credit for making it such is due to the activities of this single woman."

Kate did not stop here; the article pertaining to a department of charities contained references to "his" or "her" office. She resigned as matron of the Provident Association and announced as Democratic candidate for Commissioner of Charities and Corrections.

Already trusted by the two largest classes of voters, farmers and labor, she became the favorite speaker for her party. She painted pictures of the wrongs of childhood, the suffering of minors without protection of law, the needs of orphans, the iniquity of sending juvenile criminals to jails, the cruelties practiced upon the insane, of sweat-shops and overwork and underpay.

Her vast audiences "thrilled to her earnest eloquence"; her rapid-fire articulation left reporters in despair.

She led her ticket by 6,000 votes. In her home county, which went Republican, her majority was 1,500.

She became the first woman to be elected head of a state department in Oklahoma, and the first woman to be elected to public office in America.

Kate was born at Geneva, Nebraska, May 23, 1879, the only child of John P. and Sheila (Mason) Bernard. Her father was a lawyer and civil engineer and an Irishman of unusual qualities of mind. Her mother died when she was eighteen months old, so her malleable years were completely in his hands. To his teachings and personality Kate attributed much of the practical wisdom which so consistently animated her in her battle for social reform:

> He was a stern man with a keen sense of justice. If I did wrong punishment came. He treated me on terms of an adult. He never threatened. He never broke a promise. He hated a lie. He never conversed on frivolous subjects. Justice was with him a passion. I have known him to prosecute a man who tried to cheat him for a small amount, and I saw him voluntarily pay more than was asked to a widow who sold us vegetables at a time when we too were very poor. He would never submit to injury, lest he teach the unscrupulous not to take advantage of those too weak to protect themselves ..

> His life was full of catacylisms, but no evidence of conflict was visible except the growing stoop of his shoulders

and his whitening hair. Twice only did I see tears. The first time was at my mother's grave. Her influence over him extended thirty-three years after she was dead. It was one of those old sweet romances, the "true loves of long ago."

Once more he shed tears when he bade me good-bye and left me alone with strangers, at the time he entered the terrible "run" for a free home in Oklahoma. I was ten years old. Continued drought brought business reverses, he refused to take bankruptcy, preferring honor and poverty, so he was facing life again, a poor man at forty-five.

He took down my little autograph album and this is what he wrote: "Let Faith, Hope and Charity be the theme of your whole life and when temptation lures you to forsake either of the three great Christian principles, remember our Saviour Jesus Christ died on the cross to redeem sinners. Your loving father, John P. Barnard."

It was two years before I saw him again. When I did, it was difficult for me to recognize him with his careworn face, furrowed brow, faded eyes and silvered hair. He had aged twenty years but he was still kind and brave . . . . It is the strength of character inherited from that great pioneer which enables me to forego love, home, and other pleasures, and become a Voice in those who suffer in the gutter of human life.

John Barnard had staked a 160-acre claim twenty miles east of Oklahoma City, near Newalla, on the principal frontier highway to

Shawnee. In a one-roomed frame shanty in the sand hills, Kate lived alone another two years, while her father practiced law in Oklahoma City and served as county surveyor to make enough money to buy bread.

These were days of desperate poverty for all Oklahoma settlers, Kate recalled, and often the best her father could send her was "fat meat, navy beans and corn meal."

But she was determined to help him get a new start. She held down the claim, and it was here that bleak loneliness and hardship welded the strength and human sympathy that enabled her to defeat the sternest opposition when finally she set forth to secure laws to decrease poverty, crime and disease.

By 1894 John Barnard was able to "prove up" on his homestead. He moved Kate to Oklahoma City where she attended St. Joseph's Academy. His reverses prevented her from going to college. But this probably had its compensatory advantages. Already there had begun to stir in her the desire to be useful in a broader sphere than bounds ordinary ambition.

After graduating from the academy, she taught in public schools. In 1904, in competion with 498 applicants, she was chosen to represent Oklahoma Territory at the Louisiana Purchase Exposition in St. Louis.

It was the greatest such exhibition so far attempted. Forty-two states and 53 foreign countries participated. Kate attended all conventions that gathered in the city to discuss sociological and humanitarian questions, and gave special attention to exhibits bearing on such work, and upon returning to Oklahoma, she began to devote her efforts to aiding the unfortunate and wretched pouring into the territory by the thousands.

Newspapers recorded her local tasks rather

sketchily until November, when she converted her home into a distributing center for gifts to the poor from clubs and societies. A single appeal brought 10,000 garments. She clothed scores of children and bought them books. Medicines and groceries were handed out. Within two years, as matron of the United Provident Association, she took care of 3,000 destitute families and placed 500 children in city schools.

At the same time, she proved herself a staunch friend of the working men, as well as their families. She obtained higher wages and many other benefits for them, and organized them into a union.

The newspapers leaped to attention. She became such a public personality that the territorial governor, Frank Frantz, gave her letters of introduction to leading sociologists and political economists of St. Louis, New York and Chicago, to learn what they had done for the care and protection of children in their workshops and factories.

"No one can deal intelligently with life," Kate said, "until he first understands how all classes live and under what conditions they make their daily bread."

With this first hand information, she returned to Oklahoma. The farmers and laborers were holding a convention at Shawnee to consider means of protecting their own interests in the organic law. This body represented 65,000 votes. Kate dropped in on the convention and stayed two days. Before she came away, she had pledged to support their measures if they would endorse her three planks in the constitution.

Next, she conferred with Honorable Jesse J. Dunn, chairman of the State Democratic Campaign Committee, and he agreed to oversee her demands in the democratic platform. She had then taken the stump for Democratic success, helping elect a large majority of Democrats to the constitutional convention and, afterwards, a democratic administration for Oklahoma.

Kate saw to it that the office of Commissioner of Charities and Corrections was no empty place that drew merely honor and a salary. She plunged immediately into the task of founding upon the constitutional planks suitable legislation embodying the most advanced sociological thought and brought leaders from throughout the country to Oklahoma to address the Legislature.

Many members of the lawmaking body did not agree with such idealism or her methods. When her proposals were defeated, she took her fight to the people by organizing a state conference on charities and corrections. She drew support from representative men and women from forty-two counties, and defeated at the polls, two years later, the speaker of the House of Representatives who fought the bill vitalizing the article of the constitution creating her own department.

Nor did she shirk the responsibilities imposed on her by the constitution. Passage of laws only marked the beginning of a turbulent life for Kate Barnard.

In 1908, she visited and inspected 325 jails, poorhouses, orphanages, rescue homes — county and municipal — and state institutions for the dependent, defective and delinquent.

In April, she descended like an avenging fury on amazed Oklahoma County officials because of what she termed "pest-house horrors." Male nurses were caring for women patients in treatments that required baths and rubdowns. Her denunciations were so scathing that women nurses were employed immediately and modern sanitation methods instituted as well.

Her investigation of the city prison at Sapulpa resulted in preferring "serious charges" against the jailer. The following week Kate returned to confer with the municipal council. They voted to move toward a higher plane of management and the charges were dismissed.

Kate pulled no punches in denouncing the management of the Choctaw County jail at Hugo, in August. She told the press

> it is rotten and stinks to high heaven — the worst I have ever inspected. Twenty-one prisoners are enclosed in a small apartment with only one window. They are literally suffocating for want of air . . . .
>
> No matter how wicked a man may be, or wicked you or I may be, God Almighty has not yet shut off our air supply, and if He, in His great wisdom, can give us our daily air and sunshine, certainly we should be equally as good to our erring brothers and sisters. There can be no excuse for locking men in a cell where they will die slowly of strangulation!

She took the county commissioners to task and called a mass meeting of citizens to protest such conditions.

Again, in a four-day investigation of the hospital for the insane at Fort Supply, Miss Barnard said: "Hell has reigned here undisturbed for ten years!"

She found patients shut up in chilly corridors and cells, dark and damp with accumulated dampness, heated with only one stove at the end of each hallway, and with transom openings six inches wide above each door "through which no warm air penetrated the cells at all." There was not one trained nurse to look after the 470 patients, and little or no attention had been given

158

to their actual or attempted cure.

Boxes of rotting matter and old empty bottles littered the filthy floors. Night buckets had not been emptied, their vile odors filling the rooms.

The asylum board met at Guthrie to air Kate's charges that "the insane at Fort Supply are regarded as guilty persons to be punished rather than helpless patients to be cared for by incompetent democratic officials."

The *State Capital* described it as

> a warm session; in fact, those who were outside the room at times thought it might be well to call out the guard . . . .
>
> The board members carefully thought — and explained — that such reports hurt the democratic party and that it was a political mistake to have made the report public.
>
> Miss Barnard exploded . . . she did not care a tinker's appropriation about its effect on the party; she wanted it to have an effect on the unfortunate insane . . . . Well loaded with her facts and figures . . . she almost drove the board from the city.

Kate demanded a change in the asylum's administration. That was in January, 1909. The following month, she prevailed on Governor Charles N. Haskell to submit legislation providing for institutional comfort and sanitation.

As far as the records show, Kate backed down only once during her career. This was at Frederick, Oklahoma.

Pat — a huge bulldog — had been put on the payroll of Tillman County as a jail guard. Jailer Walter Lynch, Pat's guardian, saw possibilities in him and transferred him from the fire station, where he had been principally an ornament, to

159

the county prison, where he became exceedingly useful.

A wire was fastened the length of the hall of cells, and to it was attached the free end of Pat's chain. Thus the dog was at liberty to patrol the entire hallway, and any inmate who attempted to escape would first have to deal with Pat.

On her regular tour of county jails, Kate entered the cell block and was promptly intercepted by Pat, who planted himself menacingly in the doorway and refused to permit her to advance another step.

She called Jailer Lynch on the carpet. Lynch explained why Pat was on duty, and Kate gave him a grade of 100 percent.

"Chances are if you'll remove that dog you'll get good grades on other things," said Miss Barnard, still trembling with fear.

The dog was removed. Kate inspected the jail and came out with a report of excellence. Then Pat returned to his beat.

Kate also faced her toughest problem that year. Oklahoma had no penitentiary or reformatory. Since 1890, convicts had been farmed out under contract to Kansas. The majority of them were confined at Lansing, where they worked in the mines. Harrowing tales of insufficient food, atrocious underground working conditions and corporal punishment took Kate to Lansing for an inspection.

Her investigations and the detailed reports she made to the governors and legislatures of both states inspired a legal battle between Kansas and Oklahoma, which resulted in breaking the contract and a general overhauling of the Kansas system.

Oklahoma constructed a temporary penitentiary at McAlester, consisting of a large stockade surrounded by a high wire fence charged with electricity. Guard towers, or shacks mounted on high posts, were built outside the fence at intervals. A large frame structure in the center of the stockade had cells for 600 men. There were approximately that many Oklahoma convicts in Lansing. The Kansas contract was not renewed.

During the next few months, fifty at a time, the prisoners were removed by train to Oklahoma and put to work constructing a permanent prison. Lansing authorities were "glad to be rid of them," and the feeling was mutual. When the last train pulled out of the Lansing yards in February, 1909, cries came from the prison car: "Whoopie-ie-ie! Good-bye old Kansas! We're off for home again. Hurray for Kate Barnard!"

Kate worked closely with Governor Haskell and the penitentiary's first warden, R.W. Dick, and many of her ideas on penal control and management were adopted. A reformatory for younger convicts was built at Granite, and a training school for incorrigible boys established at Pauls Valley.

Kate's reputation grew. She appeared before the Texas Federation of Women's Clubs in the interest of juvenile legislation and a department of charities to protect the prisoners, orphans and insane of that state. In April, 1910, she was the principal speaker before the Southern Textile Conference at Memphis, Tennessee, on the subjects of "Compulsory Education" and "Conservation of Child Life," and helped organize the Southern Sociological Congress for securing a uniform child labor law for the South.

Back in Oklahoma, she plunged into a vigorous campaign for re-election to the office of charities and corrections. She again led the ticket, receiving a plurality of 72,267 votes to 34,583.

Deciding to take one of the few vacations in her life, she went to Arizona for the winter holidays. Within a week she found herself in the midst of a campaign for the addition of indeterminate sentences and a parole and probation system in the prison laws of the state. She aided Governor George Hunt in his efforts, and the reforms were passed by the next legislature.

Later, in a speech before the City Club of New York, Kate said: "In so far as my national work has taken me, I should certainly say that Arizona leads the country at present in its penal system and treatment of prisoners."

She was in demand everywhere as a speaker upon subjects nearest her heart. She lectured before the League of Political Education of New York, at Cooper Union Institute and exclusive girls schools and colleges. She addressed the Governors Congress at Richmond in 1913 and the American section of the International Tuberculosis Conference in Washington. She was voted a member of the American Academy of Social and Political Science in recognition of her contribution to the newest doctrines of popular government, and was a member of its national committee to draft amendments for the Federal Constitution to be presented to Congress. She was the American delegate to the International Prison Congress at Rome, Italy, and to the International Tuberculosis Congress at Copenhagen, Denmark. What she accomplished was so notable as to attract inquiry from Max Nordau of France, Enrico Ferri of Italy, Munsterburg of Germany, and other leaders in statecraft.

But Kate's chief interest was Oklahoma. In 1912, she succeeded in restoring $2,000,000 to Indian orphans of the state and in prosecuting many of the guardians who were depriving them of their estates.

Her old enemies in the legislature ordered her to stop the prosecutions. Kate replied: "I will not allow politicians to dictate to me!"

She hired private attorneys and continued to prosecute those guilty of graft and thievery. The

Fourth Legislature cut off her appropriations.

This battle with the Fourth Legislature brought on nervous prostration and ruined her health. Of this bleak period in her life, she wrote:

> The dust collected in layers and the spiders came and spun their webs in my silent, vacant department in which for years Christian men and women had devoted their whole time to raising standards of life for Oklahoma's poor . . . . As I stood in the chill and gloom, I looked out the State House window and noted that winter was dropping dead petals from the trees in the yard, and I thought how like these are the dead hopes and dreams which, chilled in the bitter wind of destiny, drop lifeless at our feet.

Kate also lost her father that year, and felt suddenly alone. But she did not give up when adversity swept her. She had thousands of friends in the state. Her battle was for justice, and when the legislature adjourned, she went into the home districts of the lawmakers and retired many of them to private life.

When her second term ended in 1915, she decided not to run again. She went back east, spoke in the largest halls and churches, raised several thousand dollars and returned to fight bills in the Fifth Legislature designed to facilitate the separation of the Indians from their lands.

She circularized voters of the state and organized fighting groups in forty-three counties. When these things failed, she petitioned the legislature for the right to be personally heard. She made passionate appeals from the floors of the House and Senate in behalf of Oklahoma Indians. Failing in this, she petitioned Congress to take back jurisdiction over the state's red man.

For the next several years she worked with friends of the American Indian across the nation. In September, 1922, word reached Oklahoma that Kate was lying in a Denver hospital, and unless sufficient funds could be raised to send her to Mayo's at Rochester, she probably would die.

Prominent state newspapers announced that they would receive and forward contributions to aid this dedicated friend of the friendless. The necessary amount was collected at once.

It was not until 1925 that Kate was able to return to Oklahoma, somewhat restored to health. When she did, it was with characteristic vigor and in the middle of a fight. A move was on to amend basic planks in the constitution. She promptly jumped on and routed the selfish interests seeking to tear down child labor regulations of the state.

The discovery of oil on her farm near Newalla brought substantial returns, and the next two years she traveled the state, gathering data for a book on her life and conducting a personal campaign. She announced intentions of running for the United States Senate.

Early in January, 1930, she rented a room on the fourth floor of an Oklahoma City hotel. She worked so furiously that the noise of her typewriter disturbed other tenants, and the hotel manager had her moved to a back room on the fifth floor.

Her health was again "deplorable," and she made a will, directing that her estate be used for the establishment of a Barnard Home for the Friendless through use of her old house on West Reno. On February 20, she told friends she planned to go to an eastern hospital as soon as she could finish her autobiography.

On February 23, a Negro maid entered her

164

room and found Kate Barnard dead. She sat upright, in a fighting position, as if refusing to back off even from her final adversary. She had been desperately trying to finish the last pages of her book. It was entitled *Woman of Destiny*.

KATE BARNARD as Oklahoma's first Commissioner of Charities and Corrections.

CARTOON SUMMARY of Kate Barnard's life which appeared in the Daily Oklahoman at time of her death.

KATE BARNARD as matron of the United Provident Association of Oklahoma.

ROGUES AND RAPISTS

BOOK 4

"We do not want the blood of such
wretches on our hands!"

—General Pleasant Porter
Chief of the Creek Nation

9. The Ravaging Bucks

The Sunday afternoon quiet of July 28, 1895, in the struggling village of Okmulgee, capital of the Creek Nation, was suddenly shattered by a loud whoop and the roar of a six-shooter. Alec Berryhill, an Indian policeman, was in the drug store talking with the proprietor, Doc Bell. They glimpsed a horse and rider dash past the window. By the time they reached the doorway, the horseman had disappeared in a patch of timber at the edge of town.

Old Man Parkinson, who operated a grocery store at the corner of 7th and Morton, came running up the street. "Doc Bell," he cried, "you're needed at my place — Marshal Garrett has been shot!"

City Marshal John Garrett lay on the floor, the shadow of death on his face, a bullet in his chest near the heart and bleeding badly. He struggled to sit up as Doc Bell knelt beside him.

The doctor eased him back and did what he could to staunch the flow of blood. "Who shot you?" he asked.

The officer muttered two words: "Rufus Buck—" then lapsed into a coma. A few moments later, he was dead.

Parkinson finished the story. Rufus Buck had been in process of robbing his store when Garrett came in and commanded him to raise his hands. Instead, Buck had whirled, fired at the marshal, leaped to his horse outside and sped away.

Policeman Berryhill organized a posse and rode out to apprehend the outlaw. He knew Buck well. A half-breed member of the Euchee band, Rufus was a stocky young man of twenty-two, with wild black hair and sullen, fiendish black eyes. As a boy he had been kicked out of the old Wealaka Mission Boarding School for being unruly. His father, John Buck, a prominent Euchee politician, had done little to curb his son's sheer bravado and wantonness. Already Rufus had served time in the federal prison at Fort Smith, Arkansas, for selling whiskey in Indian Territory. He was suspected of stealing horses and cattle from local ranchers. Marshal Garrett had been keeping an eye on him. Now Garrett had been disposed of . . . .

The posse searched for Buck the rest of the afternoon and far into the night. But the countryside seemed to have swallowed him.

Frank Jones, United States deputy marshal at Checotah, reached Okmulgee the next day. He rode to the Buck residence near Wealaka, but found no one at home. He lay in wait near the place three days. Finally, Rufus' sister appeared and pulled a gun on Jones, and Jones disarmed her. But she knew nothing of where Rufus was hiding.

When the Creek Nation heard of the half-breed again, he was riding with his whiskey-peddling pals Lewis Davis, a Creek freedman, and Lucky Davis, Sam Sampson and Maomi July, Creek full bloods of the Cussetah tribal town, Tulsa. All had served terms in the Fort Smith prison for offenses committed in Indian Territory. They were as twisted as Buck himself, and cared little for the valuables they took. They cared less for the cause Rufus Buck claimed to be fighting for.

There had been wide-spread differences between full bloods and mixed bloods in the Creek tribe. Whites were entering the country by the thousands, leasing Creek lands, sneering at their methods of self-government and painting glowing pictures of statehood and the advantages of casting their burdens upon the strong shoulders of the United States. Rufus Buck, like his father, was for throwing out the white man. While John Buck carried his argument to the old rock-walled

172

Council House at Okmulgee, where the two branches of the remnant Creek sovereignty — the House of Kings and House of Warriors — held sway, Rufus claimed there was a quicker way. What he really needed was an excuse to shed blood and to pillage.

He had begun by robbing Parkinson's store and killing City Marshal Garrett.

For the next thirteen days, he and his cohorts would write the most horrible chapter in the annals of Indian Territory brigandage. Their campaign of terror across the Creek Nation would make the notorious Cook, Starr and Dalton gangs, which preceeded them, look like Sunday school superintendents. They would go down as the meanest, dirtiest little band of outlaws in America.

Buck became their leader. Not because he had brains, but because he seemed to be the most moronic and depraved of the five. They made no attempt to conceal their criminal activity and thieved so often they began to make a joke of it and play cruel tricks on their victims . . .

While Deputy Jones searched for Buck near Wealaka, Mary Wilson, the widow of a tenant farmer, was moving her household goods to another farm a few miles north. Mrs. Wilson was driving the lead wagon, followed by her 14-year-old son, Charles, and Freddie Malcolm, a neighbor boy, in a second wagon, when Buck and his companions burst from the underbrush.

At sight of the woman, they halted momentarily in whispered conversation. Then they came dashing up on their steaming mounts, in sweaty, dust-caked jeans, big black and white, wide-brimmed hats and flapping vests, long-shanked spurs jingling, and six-shooters drawn.

First, they searched the woman's possessions. After taking her money and what loot appealed to them, they ordered the two boys to drive on.

173

Then Lucky Davis placed his revolver to the woman's head and ordered her out of the wagon.

"Stand by," he challenged his companions, "and watch how an expert makes love."

After he had ravished the woman, the other four nodded their approval. Then all five fired at her feet as she fled in terror. The boys finally returned to find her unconscious and near death from abuse. They took her home and summoned a doctor.

The gang had continued north. Near the little village of Natura, they met another woman named Ayers on horseback. They seized her, dragged her from the saddle and sadistically subjected her to a series of carnal "tests," "experiments," and "competitions." When she was barely conscious and only half alive, Buck yelled, "Let's ride!" and the band galloped off in search of new victims.

Eight miles further, on Berryhill Creek, they met Jim Staley riding a fine horse. Buck suggested a trade. Staley refused, and Buck knocked him from the saddle with the butt of his Winchester.

Staley writhed in the dust, blood running from his head, begging them to spare his life and take the animal. His desperate pleas entertained the thugs for a few moments. Then Buck became bored.

"I'll just blow off his damned head!"

July suggested: "Let's take a vote."

The gang voted — two for killing him, three to let him live. So Buck took his horse and saddle, fifty dollars and a gold watch, and left him bleeding on the trail.

After dark, the gang reached the home of a white renter named Gus Chambers, on Duck Creek, to steal fresh horses. Chambers stood them off with a shotgun. They "filled his house with lead," while the farmer's wife and his small son hid under the bed, but the outlaws rode off without the horses.

Sweeping southeast across the Cussetah, they reached the U-Bar ranch on Grave Creek shortly after daybreak, August 4. Benton Callahan, the ranch owner, and his hired man, Sam Houston, were moving some cattle downstream to new pasture.

The gang burst over a ridge, firing their rifles. They shot Houston's horse from under him. Houston tried to escape on foot, and Buck brought him down with a bullet through the lungs.

Buck's second shot burned alongside Callahan's head, taking off the top of his left ear. As the gang swept up around him, covering him with their weapons, Buck recognized the rancher. Callahan's father had been superintendent at Wealaka Mission when Buck had been kicked out of the school for unruly conduct.

"If I'd known it was you," the outlaw snarled, "I'd have killed you too!"

He took Callahan's horse and saddle, two dollars from his pockets, and his boots. Then the gang rode off at breakneck speed to the northwest.

The hired man and his horse were dead, the cattle had stampeded, and the rancher was barefooted. It was later afternoon before he could obtain help and a wagon to take Houston's body to Checotah.

Deputy Jones led a posse to Grave Creek. With darkness coming on, Jones was unable to find the gang's trail until the next morning, August 5. On that date, the unholy quintet reached the home of Henry Hassan between Duck and Snake creeks, twenty miles south of Sapulpa.

Hassan was an honest, hard-working farmer, barely able to support his wife Rosetta, a kindly woman of thirty, her aged mother, and three small children. All were seated beneath an arbor preparing fruit for the family larder when the Bucks rode through the front gate. Living in a secluded area where travelers seldom passed, they had not heard of the gang's depredations.

Hassan greeted them pleasantly, and asked if they were hunting.

"Sort of," Buck replied, and asked for water.

Hassan arose and started to the well for a fresh pail when he noticed that one of the outlaws was Lewis Davis. Hassan had built a snug, split-rail fence around his place, and a few weeks previously, had asked Davis to please close the gates when he passed through the farm. Davis, cursing, had told him that he had "more important things to do" and "I oughta tear down the whole fence." He could only guess what ill will Davis bore him now.

He set down the pail and started backing toward the corner of the house, hoping to reach cover, then enter a side door over which hung his Winchester. He reached the corner safely and ran towards the door, but was stopped by Maomi July, who already had entered the front of the cabin and, securing the rifle, now brushed his face with its muzzle. Sam Sampson ran up and covered him with a six-shooter.

With vile oaths, the pair hustled him back to the arbor. Rufus Buck shoved him into a chair. "Make another move," he warned, "and we'll blow your brains out both ears!" Turning to Mrs. Hassan, he ordered: "Cook us a good meal, woman, and be damn' quick about it!"

The aged mother shushed the frightened children. Inside the cabin, Rosetta put more wood in the stove and hurriedly prepared meat and eggs and black coffee.

While Lewis Davis guarded Hassan, the rest of the gang rifled the house, appropriating $5.95, a suit of clothing, baby dresses, various articles of feminine apparel, and whatever else struck their fancy. They snickered like imps from damnation and cavorted about with the undergarments of the poor woman.

Hunkered at the table, they gulped platters of food and coffee, staring at Mrs. Hassan in ominous silence. Their foulest crime was just beginning. The meal finished, they came out to stand guard over Hassan, the old mother and the children, while Lewis Davis went in to dinner.

The smelly, sullen freedman wolfed down his food quickly, eyeing Mrs. Hassan's well-proportioned figure. His appetite appeased, he told her: "You go to the barn with me."

Rosetta pleaded with him not to take her away from her husband and babies. Davis snarled: "We'll kill your husband and throw the God damn' brats in the creek!"

Believing it was the only way to save her family, the woman obeyed. She walked to the barn, while Lewis Davis held his six-shooter to the back of her head. Inside, he ordered her to lie down . . . .

What happened afterward was repeated, one, two, three, four times, each of the slobbering, sweating brutes taking his turn while the others remained ready to send lead crashing through the head of her husband if he attempted to remonstrance.

Finally they mounted their horses, ordering Hassan to remove his boots and walk ahead of them to the creek. Here, for another half hour, they amused themselves by making him dance, firing random shots at his toes and heels to keep the jig lively, then compelled him to wrestle and fight them and dragged him in the water. And when he could stand the exertion no longer and dropped in a faint from sheer exhaustion, Rufus Buck awakened him with a couple of back-handed blows and the parting admonition: "If you ever appear against us, we'll come back and kill you."

To his companions, Buck remarked: "After this day, other whites will think ten times before entering this territory to work the soil of another Indian!"

The rapists-robbers whooped in agreement as they rode off.

A few minutes later, a neighbor driving along the creek discovered the bruised and beaten farmer. Hassan crawled painfully into the wagon, and they drove quickly to help his wife. The mother, virtually helpless from age's infirmities, was still in the yard, sobbing and trying to comfort the screaming children. Rosetta was missing.

"Where is she?" Hassan cried. "Where did she go?"

The old mother could only shake her head and point toward the cornfield. There Hassan found his wife, babbling half out of her mind from apprehension and, with the ragged remnant of her bloody skirt, trying to cover her shame. Gently he carried her to the house while the neighbor went for a doctor.

Word of their ordeal spread like wildfire, adding fuel to the fever of shock and horror that already swept the countryside. White men everywhere vowed such bitter, fierce vengeance that it must have shaken the old gallows of "Hanging Judge" Isaac C. Parker's court in session at Fort Smith.

S. Morton Rutherford, United States Marshal for the Northern District of Indian Territory, at Muskogee, ordered every available deputy on the Buck gang's trail. Within hours, thirty armed manhunters, equipped to spend weeks in the field if necessary, were hounding the inhuman wretches. Even the natives vowed that wild animals like the Bucks must die, and General

178

Pleasant Porter, Chief of the Creeks, dispatched his Indian Lighthorse (national police) under Captain Edmund Harry, in full force.

They scoured the country two hard days and nights, while Buck kept his thugs on the move, through the Tuskegee hills, across the Deep Fork of the Canadian, down the timbered valley of Wolf Creek.

On August 9, the gang looted the little sawmill village of Norberg after driving nearly twenty persons down the creek, blazing at their heels with Winchesters, then robbed Orcutt's store near McDermott, and doubled back west of Okmulgee to rob the general store of a man named Knobble. They bound Knobble hand and foot, stuffed two grain sacks with clothing, coffee, meat, canned goods, tobacco and ammunition, and fled back into the hills.

This was great fun.

But it didn't last. At noon next day they halted in a little glade at the base of a flat-topped hill near Preston to rest their horses and began arguing over how the plunder should be divided.

Rufus Buck didn't like it. He told his thugs, since he was the leader, that he would divide the loot and take first choice. The others didn't like that. They started quarrelling again. At that moment they were sighted by Deputy Marshals Sam Haynes and N.B. Irwin and Captain Harry with his Indian police.

The officers attacked from three sides. So sudden and unexpected was the onslaught, the renegades had no time to mount. With muffled oaths, they seized their rifles and ammunition and fled to the top of the plateau, pumping volleys at the pursuers below.

The heated battle continued for an hour. The officers spread around the base of the hill, firing and moving upward behind rocks and bushes as safety permitted. The outlaws, flattened around the rim, kept up a rattling reply. When their weapons were empty, they would retire to the center of the knob, reload, creep back to the edge and open fire again.

Shortly after one o'clock, just as federal court convened, a dispatch reached Fort Smith that the posse had the Buck gang surrounded. Their vicious acts had filled the border press; now the news of the possibility of their capture flashed to every nook and cranny of the city.

It reached the four hundred persons who packed the corridors and the courtroom to hear the petty cases being tried, and instantly everything was confusion. A bailiff whispered the news to Judge Parker. He nodded, smiled, then quietly called for order.

The cases proceeded, but the eager uneasiness grew. Then came a second dispatch. As the gunfire echoed through the countryside, nearly a hundred citizens who were hunting the gang had rushed to the scene to join the fight. There was no chance for the Bucks to escape!

The bustle in the courtroom increased. Attorneys forgot to ask questions and witnesses to answer them. Again and again, Judge Parker called for order. But his tone was kindly, and he seemed to join with the crowd in secret exultation. And when court finally adjourned that evening, everyone hurried to the telegraph and newspaper officers to learn of any later developments in the battle.

Marshal Rutherford had hurried from Muskogee with a fresh posse, reaching the scene at dusk. The constant pumping of lead with the accompanying flashes gave the appearance of a blaze of fire and smoke hung so thickly over the knob that the belligerents were sometimes hidden from each other. The assaulting parties, lying full length on the ground and shooting upward with nothing left but grass roots for concealment, had almost reached the rim of the plateau.

Finally, an old Indian named Shansey rose bravely to his feet and yelled: "I've had enough of this; let's stand up and fight like men!"

He shoved a dynamite cartridge into his rifle, intended to stand only the force of exploding gunpowder, lifted the weapon and pulled the trigger.

The explosive struck the rim where the gang's fire was concentrated. A piece of the shell cut Rufus Buck's cartridge belt. As it dropped to the ground, he threw down his Winchester and fled. This demoralized the others and they ran pell mell down the opposite side of the hill into the arms of Rutherford's posse. All five outlaws were captured and put in chains.

Bonfires glowed over the countryside as crowds of people, who a few days before would rather have met Satan himself, eagerly gathered for a glimpse of the terrible Bucks. Muffled threats were made. Soon lynching was being talked of openly. The Creeks had been accused repeatedly by whites of laxity in upholding the law and failure to assist in its prosecution. They smarted under the accusation, and here was an opportunity to work summary punishment at rope's end.

Marshal Rutherford told them: "You cannot have the prisoners without a fight, and my men will shoot straight. The life of one of you is not worth the lives of all of them!"

Calmly, dispassionately, he referred to the austere, white-haired Judge Parker as "a certain punisher of crime," and added: "I promise you they will be tried by him."

The English speaking members of the mob quieted down, but many of the Indians did not fully understand his statement. Whereupon General Porter explained in Creek that the outlaws would not be surrendered without bloodshed, and said: "We do not want the blood of such wretches on our hands!"

The Indians moved back, gathering around their fires in ominous silence. Meanwhile, Rutherford consulted earnestly with the prisoners. He told them if they remained there they would be lynched; that, in the darkness, he believed the officers could easily steal them through the lines, except for the clanking of their heavy chains. It is a matter of record that these renegades, who had so little regard for the lives of others, but valued their own so highly, picked up the chains and carried them a full half mile without a sound. From this point they were rushed fifty miles to Muskogee, where they were hastily loaded on a convenient train.

The grim cargo reached Fort Smith on Sunday morning, August 12. Hundreds of persons jammed the Missouri-Pacific depot on the banks of the Arkansas at the end of Garrison avenue for their first view of these "fiends in human form."

No time was lost. Garrison avenue ran southeasterly. Three blocks from the depot stood the gate to the old government barracks enclosure, from which a path led diagonally south to the federal jail. The crowd fell back as the prisoners came off the train, chains clanking at every step. The marshals headed for the sidewalk, some leading the way, the others bringing up the rear. The crowd closed in and followed only after the procession had marched a safe distance. Somebody ran to a nearby church and began ringing a bell. Within a few minutes every church bell in the city was tolling the news that this fierce band had been brought under the majesty of the law.

During the week, Assistant U.S. District Attorney J.B. McDonough gathered a mass of evi-

182

dence concerning their crimes. The rape of Rosetta Hassan, the most vile of their deeds, was laid before the grand jury and an indictment returned August 19. Their trial was held September 23. When the story of their savagery and brutality had been presented, William M. Cravens, one of five attorneys appointed for the defense, arose and stated, simply, "May it please the court and you gentlemen of the jury . . . I have nothing to say." The jury returned a guilty verdict within three minutes.

Two days later, the gang appeared before Judge Parker for sentencing. The judge was a big man, over six feet tall and weighing 200 pounds. His deep voice rolled to the corridors and every corner of the courtroom:

"The verdict is an entirely just one, and one that must be approved by all lovers of virtue . . . . The Lawmakers of the United States have deemed your offense equal in enormity and wickedness to murder. It has been proven beyond question; the manner of its commission leaves no ground for the extension of sympathy . . . .

"I sentence you, Rufus Buck, to be hanged by the neck until dead. May God, whose laws you have broken, and before whose tribunal you must now appear, have mercy on your soul!"

He then pronounced the sentence upon each of the remaining four, and set October 31 as the date of execution. Lucky Davis sneered. The others "exhibited no sign of emotion and seemed to care nothing for it."

Buck appealed to the Supreme Court on grounds that, if given an opportunity, he could prove an alibi. But the higher court affirmed the decision of the Fort Smith court, and the members of the gang were re-sentenced to be hanged on July 1, 1896.

The five sat on a bench on the gibbet and glanced over its hideous paraphernalia as Unit-

ISAAC CHARLES PARKER, the "Hanging Judge" of Fort Smith, Arkansas, sentenced the Buck gang to death. They were hanged as a quintet on the Fort Smith gallows, July 1, 1896.

BUCK GANG in chains (L to R: Maomi July, Sam Sampson, Rufus Buck,
Lucky Davis and Lewis Davis).

185

ed States Marshal George J. Crump of the Western District of Arkansas read the death warrants. Then he asked each in turn, "Have you anything to say?"

"No," they replied, one by one, till he came to Lewis Davis. "I want to be hanged by myself," Davis said. The request was denied.

Crump motioned the men to stand on the hinged trap and the dangling nooses were placed around their necks. Gazing over the crowd of witnesses, Buck saluted them. Lucky Davis saw one of his relatives standing in the corner of the yard and called, "Goodbye."

The black caps were adjusted, the lever pulled. The cumbersome trap dropped with a heavy "chug." Out in the Creek Nation people breathed easy again, and all that was left of the ravaging Bucks hung limp and quivering.

10. Mad Artist of McAlester

As the visitor passes through the Oklahoma State Penitentiary at McAlester, he enters the great prison rotunda. He pauses, eyes lifting from the gray floor to the long tiers of cell blocks crawling up to the steel-girded dome.

For a moment he stares curiously, almost startled by four large paintings that adorn the walls at the compass points of the high circular room.

The fine canvases are approximately sixteen feet wide and ten feet high. One is a Biblical scene of Joseph, Mary and the Christ child fleeing into Egypt. The others are temporal reproductions of the First Thanksgiving in America, Napoleon at Waterloo, and one titled "Culture," depicting the American Indian studying the alphabet.

The paintings, strange for a prison, are looked upon with pride by the inmates, because they were produced by one of them—a murderer named Conrad Maas.

"He was German," one lifer tells you. "He spent twenty-six years here. Three governors offered to pardon him, but he refused, preferring to live and die behind these walls in a little studio rigged up for him in the loft of the mule barn."

Then, as if an afterthought, he adds: "Maas had a colorful background. He was the strangest man I've ever known. A real loner. Seldom spoke to anybody. Seemed all froze up inside and couldn't let go. But you got to know him when you understood the emotions which led up to the crime that put him here . . . ."

Maas' story began in Blaine County a couple of years after that part of Oklahoma Territory was settled by the "run" of April 19, 1892. Blaine County consisted of most of the northeast portion of the Cheyenne and Arapaho Indian reservation. At the time of the opening, it was designated county "C" by the government, and Watonga, named for the Arapaho chief, Black Coyote, was laid out as the county seat. Later, the county was named for James G. Blaine of Maine, speaker of the U.S. House of Representatives and unsuccessful candidate for president.

Although sparsely populated, it was rich country with triple blessings — fertile sandy loam soil, scenic beauty and plenty of water — bound on the northeast by the Cimarron River, traversed in the center by the North Canadian, and bound on the south by the South Canadian. There was an immense crop of wheat, corn and cotton, and the prospect for the next year's crop could not have been better when Maas arrived with his wife, a buxom blonde little creature with sparkling eyes, named Martha.

They took a claim in the southern part of the county near Bridgeport, a crossing on the South Canadian in the Wichita Indian reservation.

Maas planted corn and grain sorghums and built a sod dugout in the side of a hill.

Watonga had a population of about 500. Its early frame buildings were being replaced by stone and brick structures. Maas took a job in town as a brick mason. Frequently his wife accompanied him to the county seat to do their shopping.

His difficulty in adjusting to democratic ways caused a great deal of speculation. He was tight-lipped, unfriendly, contemptuous of others in the region, especially his cowboy and Indian neighbors across the Canadian. When he did speak it was with a guttural, almost unintelligible accent that carried a haughty insolence. His saving graces were his unflagging industry and his obvious love for his pretty wife. They walked hand-in-hand on the streets, and at home were often seen in the fields together.

Martha adored her bearded, beak-nosed, taciturn husband. His attitude toward others embarrassed her not in the least. She spoke English little better than Maas, but she laughed and chatted with the townswomen and invited some of them to her home. Few accepted. Maas' insolent glances made it plain he did not care for company.

"He just wants to keep his young bride to himself," was the way people summed it up. "He likes the country, but has no time for those who live in it. Reckon he has a right to be left alone."

But Maas continued to be a topic for gossip, especially after he began receiving letters from the old country. Some bore return addresses of a Count Von Maas and a Count Von Hohenstein. One letter bore the imperial stamp of the Emperor in Berlin.

Apparently Conrad Maas was a high-born member of the German Hohenzollerns. The Von Hohenstein clan was related to the Hohenzollerns, the ruling dynasty. Even the Blaine County settlers knew that. The way Maas carried himself stiffly erect, with squared shoulders and precise tread, led them to believe he had been in the German army before coming to America.

Maas volunteered no information, and people asked no questions.

The months passed and he grew sullen and brooding. As more letters arrived, his temper became as short and vicious as a demon's. His wife ceased to accompany him to Watonga, they quarreled bitterly, and he walked his fields alone, restlessly.

In town, he squabbled with his fellow workers, and horse-whipped a street lounger named Indian Jack for derisively referring to him as "the Count." Some cowboys rushed from the saloon and made Jack put up his knife.

As Maas coiled his whip and returned to his buggy, one of the men drawled: "Your private affairs is none of Jack's business. But he ain't entirely at fault. Your high-minded ways brought part of it on yourself."

Still seething with anger, Maas glared down at the speaker. Then he said, "As you say, my private affairs iss none of his business." He spoke with his guttural accent so all could hear. With an arrogant glance at the crowd, he clucked to his team and drove off toward home.

A few minutes later, Sheriff J.K. Kenny picked up Indian Jack. The redman promised there would be no further trouble.

The sheriff's deputy, J.D. Marion, wasn't so sure, however. "Jack is half Cheyenne. If Maas ain't careful, he'll stick that knife clean through him some day."

"If anything happens to Maas," the sheriff replied, "Jack will be the first man we'll jail."

Maas quit his town job. He was not seen in

Watonga for some time.

On December 5, 1898, a bitterly cold day, he drove into the livery stable and told the owner he would like to board his team while he was away on urgent business in Kansas City. He carried a suitcase and seemed worried.

Asked about his wife, he said, "It iss not possible for her to go." Then he confided to the liveryman, "She iss going to have a baby."

"Do you think she will be all right?"

Maas nodded. "I will be gone only a week — maybe a little longer."

News soon spread of his wife's delicate condition and Maas' departure. A heavy snow began falling that afternoon and continued two days. The third morning, Mrs. Nancy Banks who lived in the Maas neighborhood, came whipping her horse up to the sheriff's office. She explained that as soon as the storm broke she had gone over to look in on the German's wife. The farm appeared deserted. Cattle huddled in the shed and corral, without feed or water. No smoke came from the chimney of the dugout. Her alarm grew as she noticed there were no tracks in the snow that had drifted across the doorstep.

"I pounded on the door, but got no answer!" exclaimed the woman, still breathless and worn from her hard ride.

Sheriff Kenny and Deputy Marion rode to the dugout and broke open the door. Martha Maas lay dead on the floor in a pool of dried blood. She had been shot twice with a shotgun, one load entering her left side and ranging downward, the other striking her under the left ear. The weapon lay beside her. Her clothes were badly torn and everything in the dugout indicated that a hard fight had taken place before the murder was committed. The dried blood and absence of tracks showed it had happened before or during the storm.

"I've been afraid of something like this," Deputy Marion said. "A lot of people hate Maas, but only a polecat would take it out on his wife."

The sheriff nodded. "You high-tail it back to town and send out the undertaker and coroner. I'll finish the investigation. Meanwhile, pick up Indian Jack."

By noon, the coroner had made his examination and the body was removed to Watonga. More than a score of neighbors and townsmen spread over the countryside to help search for clues.

Like Kenny and Marion, they directed their suspicions first toward the enemies of the woman's husband. They also recalled the trouble he'd had with wild cowboys passing through from the Wichita reservation. A few pointed to the bad characters along the Canadian and the fact that none of them were beyond attacking a lone woman. Martha Maas had tried to defend herself with the shotgun and one of them had killed her.

The investigation might have gone off on a dozen tangents, except for two things: Every item of Maas' wearing apparel was missing, indicating that he had gone for good, and one of the letters he had received from Germany apparently had been overlooked in packing.

Kenny took the missive to a Watonga merchant who could read several languages. "Can you tell me what it says?" he asked.

The man scanned the letter and his brows puckered gravely. "Conrad Maas is a high-born gentleman, all right, a friend of Wilhelm himself. Both are members of a secret society called *Order of Eagles*. He was in the army, too, holding the rank of Major. Count Von Maas is a brother and Count Von Hohenstein an uncle. They are urging him to return to his homeland. Wilhelm has even agreed to restore his commission if he gives up Martha Muller."

The sheriff asked, "Who's Martha Muller?"

"Must have been his wife's maiden name. Seems Maas was exiled for marrying a commoner." The merchant flipped a page, then added: "Here it is — this passage: 'When this ridiculous fascination has passed, you will find yourself in need of your own country and your own kind. You understand, of course, that the girl will never be allowed to re-enter Germany.' " The merchant concluded: "Seems Martha Maas was the root of all his trouble — caused him to desert his command and come to America."

It cleared up a lot of things for the sheriff. No wonder Maas had been so anti-social. It certainly was a long hop from the gay lights and laughter of a Berlin ballroom to breaking sod on a Blaine County claim. Kenny thrust the letter back in his pocket.

Marion was waiting for him at the office. The deputy had been unable to locate Indian Jack. "He left camp three days ago with a jug of whiskey and a couple of squaws and went up to that Cheyenne village on the Canadian."

It was just as well. "I don't think he killed Martha Maas," Kenny said. He showed the deputy the letter and explained its contents. "Maas wanted Martha Muller enough to desert the army and marry beneath his own class. The letters came, and he got to brooding over what he had lost. He decided to return to Germany without the woman who loved and trusted him. Then she told him she was pregnant. They quarreled, and he decided to get rid of her. The day he left town, his wife was already dead."

Their job was to find Conrad Maas. The railroad agent looked surprised when the officers questioned him. Maas had not gone to Kansas at all. He had caught a train east toward El Reno and Oklahoma City.

"Probably headed straight for the East Coast to board a ship for Germany," remarked Marion. "What can we do now?"

"Notify the immigration authorities," the sheriff said. "I'll keep him from sailing if I have to call every port from New Orleans to Maine!"

On authority of a murder warrant issued by the Blaine county attorney, the federal government went into action. Within a few hours, however, Kenny called off the manhunt. A wire from the Canadian County sheriff informed him that Maas was in custody at El Reno.

The El Reno *News* of Friday, December 9, gave this account of what happened:

> Last Monday night, Conrad Maas, a well-to-do farmer (claiming to live) four miles west of Weatherford (in Custer County), rushed into El Reno and voluntarily gave himself up to the sheriff, stating that his wife had been murdered and that he had come in to escape the job. He stated that two wounds were inflicted by the discharge of both barrels of a double barreled shotgun . . . .
>
> A telegram (inquiry) was sent to the point nearest the scene of the accident.
>
> The action of Maas from the time he came in was that of an insane man. He wrote telegrams to his mother in German and to the Pinkerton detective agency. In the morning he said he didn't know whether his wife had been murdered or not, that he believed she had been kidnapped about Thanksgiving time, and after another day had passed without any evidence (from Weatherford) corroborating his statement, it came to be quite generally be-

lieved that the man was insane and proceedings were contemplated for his removal to the asylum at Norman.

Later events, however, have established the fact that the man's wife was found dead in the family home near Bridgeport and under circumstances that made his original story very probably the truth. This placed the killing in Blaine county, and of course that county has jurisdiction of the case.

When Kenny and Marion called for Maas, he refused to accompany them. They were forced to put him in handcuffs and chains to return him to Watonga.

He admitted leaving Germany because of his love for young Martha and the pressure from relatives to free himself from the "taint of common blood" and thereby "vindicate" himself in the eyes of his noble clan. But he staunchly denied having murdered his wife. However, when confronted with the statement he made to the El Reno sheriff, he became confused and stammering.

The Watonga *Republican* of December 14 commented that Maas

is trying to play crazy. A man who would commit such a deed has more hell than insanity in him.

The Insanity Board of Blaine County thought so, too. In February, 1899, the grand jury found an indictment for murder, and at the October term of court he was found guilty and sentenced to life imprisonment. Territorial prisoners were "farmed out" to Kansas, and Maas was confined at Lansing.

He did not stay long. Prison psychiatrists examined him and declared him insane. The

Blaine County prosecutor took exception, arguing that he was a malingerer and the question of his sanity had been decided by the jury that convicted him. However, Kansas returned him under terms of the contract which permitted it to refuse insane convicts.

But Oklahoma stuck to its guns. For the next few years, Maas was kept in the Watonga jail.

During this period his relatives, through the German consul at St. Louis, Friedrich C. Rieloff, prevailed upon Governor Frank Frantz to consider a pardon on grounds that Maas was insane. Dr. H.W. Hermann, a specialist in nervous and mental diseases, and one of the leading alienists of the country, was sent to Watonga by Rieloff to examine Maas. At the hearing before Frantz, Dr. Hermann testified that in his opinion the man was insane, but admitted that sometimes insane persons were responsible for their acts. Rieloff's efforts were in vain.

After statehood, the legislature finally provided for the erection of a penitentiary at McAlester, and Oklahoma's convicts were transferred from Lansing during the winter of 1908-1909. Convicts in county jails were transferred during the spring of 1910. Conrad Maas entered McAlester on March 27 as Number 1770.

Shortly after his arrival, he was assigned to a detail to paint the prison mule barn. While at work, he managed to smuggle a large brush and some paint to his cell. With bits of wood and bristles from the stolen brush, he fashioned small art brushes. He had studied painting during his early years at the University of Berlin, but gave up the hobby at the beginning of his military career. He now turned to it as escape from the realities of prison life.

He worked secretly, at night, mixing shades, experimenting. His first painting was on a window curtain in his cell.

It was so striking when discovered that the warden, instead of disciplining him, gave him permission to paint in leisure hours when his work was done.

Word spread as his skill increased. Substantial offers were made for some of his works, but Maas wasn't interested. He donated them to churches. Many were hung in the prison dining hall. Others he sold to guards and fellow convicts at $5 each.

As he perfected his technique, he was provided with a studio in the loft of an old barn. White rats, pigeons and cats became his only companions. He had a small door cut for the pigeons and cats to come and go. Art students came to study his work and feature stories appeared in the newspapers. They called him the "Mad Artist of McAlester."

In 1923, due to public sentiment and belief that he had sufficiently expiated for his crime, Governor Jack Walton offered him a parole.

Maas declined. Where would he go? The first World War had wrecked Germany. Life there was no longer attractive. His relatives and friends were gone. If he left prison, he could not paint. "This is all of life," he said.

A second offer came from Governor Henry S. Johnston, in 1927, a third from Governor William H. "Alfalfa Bill" Murray in 1934. Maas refused both. "I wish they would leave me alone. My sentence iss for life. I will stay until it iss ended."

He was nearing eighty, and there was so much to do. He had produced over fifty paintings in twenty-six years. The four larger works were almost completed.

Sunday afternoon, April 5, 1936, Maas was found in his studio, lapsed into a coma. The end came a few hours later in the prison hospital. Without speaking, he died as he had lived, silent and alone.

His grave in the prison cemetery bears only a simple marker, but his canvases on the rotunda walls keep alive his legend.

CONRAD MAAS as #1770, Oklahoma State Penitentiary at McAlester, 1910.

WATONGA, named for an Arapaho chief, Black Coyote, as it looked at time of Maas' arrival shortly after the opening of the Cheyenne-Arapaho reservation to white settlement in 1892.

ON A BITTERLY cold day in December, 1898, Maas drove into Watonga
livery stable (building at extreme right) and asked owner to board his
team while he was away on urgent business in Kansas City.

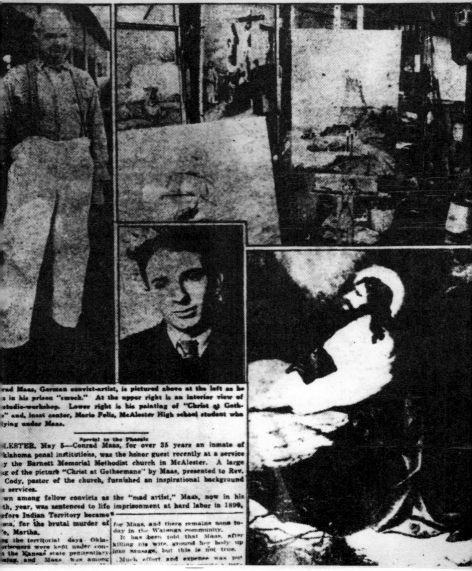

rad Maas, German convict-artist, is pictured above at the left as he
a in his prison "smock." At the upper right is an interior view of
studio-workshop. Lower right is his painting of "Christ at Goth-
" and, inset center, Mario Polis, McAlester High school student who
ying under Maas.

Special to the Phoenix

LESTER, May 5—Conrad Maas, for over 35 years an inmate of
klahoma penal institutions, was the honor guest recently at a service
y the Barnett Memorial Methodist church in McAlester. A large
g of the picture "Christ at Gethsemane" by Maas, presented to Rev.
Cody, pastor of the church, furnished an inspirational background
services.

wn among fellow convicts as the "mad artist," Maas, now in his
th, year, was sentenced to life imprisonment at hard labor in 1899,
fore Indian Territory became   for Maas, and there remains none to-
a, for the brutal murder of   day in the Watonga community.
, Martha.   It has been told that Maas, after
g the territorial days. Okla- killing his wife, ground her body up
isoners were kept under con-   into sausage, but this is not true.
the Kansas state penitentiary   Much effort and expense was put
ng, and Maas was among

**IN PRISON, Maas produced over fifty paintings. He refused parole of-
fers from two governors, art students came to study his work, and newspapers called him the "Mad Artist of McAlester."**

200

SILVER STARS
AND SUDDEN GUNS

BOOK 5

"He was by training and at heart a Quaker, but if a man smote him on one cheek and he turned the other to be smitten, the smiter would be looking into the business end of his six-shooter."

—John D. Miles
Agent of the Cheyenne-Arapaho

11. Quaker Marshal

Looking back at him across the years, it is difficult to understand how anyone could have thought him dangerous. Small in build, blue-eyed, quiet-faced, he appeared harmless enough. His dress was any clothing he could afford, topped by a flat-crowned, broad-brimmed black hat symbolic of his exact physical and mental make-up. Agent John D. Miles, who brought him to Darlington, in western Indian Territory, in 1872, said: "He was by training and at heart a Quaker, but if a man smote him on one cheek and he turned the other to be smitten, the smiter would be looking into the business end of his six-shooter."

He was Benjamin F. Williams, deputy United States marshal. His purpose was to preserve order on the Cheyenne and Arapaho reservations.

The Indians, however, were slow to bestow confidence in any white man who had not proven himself in their searching estimation. They doubted that he could deliver to the reckless violator of the law the necessary restraint, even if it transgressed his Quaker principles. They called him "Blackbeard" because of his full head of heavy dark brown hair and whiskers that covered his face and neck.

The path Ben Williams followed to his appointment as a peace officer was a rocky one. He was born in 1837 near Salem, Ohio, and educated in local district schools. His parents were members of the Society of Friends, and he and his seven brothers and sisters were reared strictly in this faith. When he was eleven, his mother died. Although numerous Quaker families lived in this portion of Ohio, Ben's ancestors were ever pioneers. From the time they left the Quaker colonies of Pennsylvania, they always had pushed westward. After his mother's death, Ben accompanied an older brother, John, and two of his sisters to Muscatine, Iowa. His father, Doctor Dearman Williams, and the rest of the family followed a few months later. The next four years were spent in establishing a new home on this fringe of settlement.

Ben's introduction to real pioneer conditions came in 1859, when he joined the Pike's Peak gold rush and crossed the plains to Colorado with a young neighbor named Collins. The youths sluice-mined in Graham Gulch until winter, then hunted and trapped out the season.

In Colorado he developed all the resourcefulness of a frontiersman and a remarkable proficiency with firearms. His favorite weapon was the rifle. Whether he was influenced by his wild mining camp associations or merely followed the dictates of his independent disposition, he cut loose from the faith of the quiet, peaceable people in which he had been reared and went his own way. When the Civil War erupted, he returned home and enlisted in the 5th Iowa Cavalry.

Ben served faithfully through all non-commissioned grades and was promoted to lieutenant. He was with Grant's army at the capture of Forts Donelson and Henry and participated in the Battle of Pittsburg Landing, where he was taken prisoner. He was confined at Winston, Libby and, finally, Andersonville.

Six months later, Sherman began his march to the sea. Andersonville lay in the path of the Federal advance and had to be evacuated. In the confusion, Ben managed to escape. He was trailed by bloodhounds and came within a hair's breadth of recapture before reaching Union lines. Weak and emaciated from the rigors of malaria and imprisonment, he was furloughed home to recuperate. The war ended and he never returned to service. He rented some land near Muscatine and engaged in farming until called to

Darlington.

Brinton Darlington, for whom the agency was named, had lived at Salem, Ohio. A leading business man and a most earnest member of the Society of Friends, he knew the Williams family well. They had come to him as their spiritual counselor when they removed to Iowa. In 1869, President Grant appointed Brinton Darlington agent of the Cheyenne and Arapaho Indians, then being permanently located in Indian Territory.

The treaty with the Cheyenne and Arapaho provided that certain artisans and shops be maintained for their benefit. Agent Darlington, knowing John Williams to be conscientious, industrious, skillful and discreet, had hired him as agency blacksmith, and hired Edwin Williams, Ben's younger brother, as agency engineer.

Agent Darlington died in 1872, and John D. Miles, another Quaker, was appointed to fill the vacancy. Miles had taught school in Ohio and operated a milling business at Wabash, Indiana. In the winter of 1868-69 he served as agent for the Kickapoo tribe then living on a reservation near Atchison, Kansas. In 1871 he was sent as a special commissioner to the Republic of Mexico to secure the removal of the Mexican Kickapoo back to the United States.

Arriving at Darlington, he found the Cheyenne-Arapaho reservation overrun with white outlaws stealing horses from the Indians and plundering freight wagons on the Chisholm Trail. He asked the Department of the Interior for authority to employ a competent man to run down these outlaws and see that they were prosecuted. The authority was granted. John Williams, who had become Miles' principal advisor, recommended his brother Ben.

Ben had recovered his health on the Iowa farm. His sickness had left him bony and thin, but he was quick and active, and in the service had learned to handle all kinds of weapons. In addition, his appointment would keep agency operations in Quaker hands. He was sent for at once.

The entire Indian Territory at that time was under the exclusive jurisdiction of the Federal District Court for the Western District of Arkansas. In order that there might be no question as to his authority to serve writs, make arrests and hold prisoners, Ben was issued a deputy's commission by the United States Marshal at Fort Smith. His range would be all that country west of the Five Civilized Tribes extending to the Texas panhandle and No Man's Land. His job was to bring law violators from across the rivers, hills and valleys to Darlington. From there they could be transported by stage up the Chisholm to Wichita, thence east by rail across Kansas into Missouri and south to Fort Smith. For this service he would receive the munificent salary of $100 per month out of which he paid his own expenses.

Ben stuffed his coat pocket with warrants and went to the horse corral at the rear of the agency buildings. He didn't take time to let down the bars. He placed his hands on the top rail, which was about chin high, and vaulted up and over like a cat. Saddling his pony, he leaped astride with a bound, cleared the fence in a running jump and rode off across the North Canadian.

A Colt's .45 was strapped to his waist. In the crook of his left arm he carried a long Henry rifle. From that position, whether riding or afoot, he had learned to make his best shots. His strike was deadly accurate and swift as a rattlesnake's. With the Colt's six-shooter, he fired straight from the shoulder — fancy hip shots seldom hit the mark.

Of all the outlaws lurking in the wilderness

and along the trails to Darlington none was more dangerous than a desperado with the sobriquet of "Wild Bill." Since the Indians wanted proof of his ability, and his work would be so in accord with their own interests, Ben went directly to them for any possible information. He learned that Wild Bill had been seen on Deer Creek, only a few miles from the Cheyenne village.

Ben cut his sign in late evening, heading southwest in a course quartering the setting sun. His warrant for the outlaw read "fugitive," which meant he could be brought in upright or horizontally. Though neither man saw the other, it soon became apparent that the desperado knew he was being followed. The race ended at nightfall, temporarily.

At the crack of dawn Williams was in the saddle again. He passed the site of the hunted man's camp shortly after daylight. Afterwards, he maneuvered to keep from view in brushy lowlands and depressions off the direct trail. Reaching the Washita, he spotted his man beyond the river. Wild Bill turned into a trail that led down the valley. At mid-day, the fugitive reached a log house that had been built by a venturesome Indian trader.

Obviously the trader was not at home. The outlaw took a position in the doorway, watching the country he had traversed that morning. Between Ben and the cabin lay more than a mile of open valley.

To approach it before darkness would be pure folly. But darkness also meant that the fugitive might easily escape. Ben concealed his pony and moved to a point where he could watch his man and await developments.

In the middle of the afternoon, Wild Bill disappeared inside the house. Williams sprang to his feet. He ducked from sight again when the outlaw stepped back into the doorway.

Then he saw what had drawn the desperado's attention. Something, or someone, was moving down the trail from the northwest. After a few minutes Ben made out a man driving a covered wagon and concluded it was the trader.

Quickly he moved into action. Keeping to low ground, he led his pony to where the timber along the river would screen him. Then he mounted and raced to intercept the vehicle.

He hailed the driver and identified himself. Fortunately, the man proved cooperative. Ben outlined a plan by which he hoped to capture Wild Bill, or at least give him an opportunity to surrender.

Leaving his pony to graze, the marshal removed the tailgate and seated himself in the wagon-box under the canvas with his rifle across his knees. "When you reach the cabin," he told the trader, "swing the wagon completely around in front."

This would bring Ben face to face with the man still standing in the doorway. The rest would be up to him.

Vigilant curiosity kept Wild Bill's eyes on the vehicle as it approached, but he showed no signs of alarm. The team sprang into a trot; the brake-gear rattled and harness creaked as the wagon rose from the ruts to take the turn. The action was so natural there was no change in the outlaw's attitude, until he suddenly saw the marshal seated in the box with his rifle leveled.

"Hands up!" Ben shouted. "You're my prisoner!"

Instead of obeying the order, Wild Bill reached for his six-shooter. His hand was on the holster when Ben's rifle spoke. The bullet struck him near the heart.

He grasped the door jamb with his left hand to keep from falling and tried vainly to draw his revolver. Ben sprang from the wagon and struck his hand loose from the jamb. The outlaw fell prone in the doorway, still conscious. His eyes showed all the venom he held for the marshal as he spoke his last words:

"Damn you, Williams — you have killed me!"

Ben regretted having to take the life of Wild Bill. Agent Miles assured him that it could not have well been otherwise.

Wild Bill's disposal also removed the doubt from the minds of Indian leaders. Still they refused to bestow their friendship and confidence. For some time they had been plagued by a band of horse thieves led by a two-gunned Texan ruffian named Lee. They wondered if the marshal could break up this tough outfit.

The Lee gang totaled sixteen members. Ben had no assistance. There was a troop of cavalry from Fort Dodge in the field, but they were looking for a party of buffalo hunters they had been ordered to capture and escort out of the country. So Ben spent days away from Darlington, alone, trailing the gang as far as Red River and the panhandle, without catching up with them.

Finally he managed to arrest two of the thieves and recover some ponies stolen from Cheyenne Chief Little Robe's camp on the Canadian. He shackled the pair to the horns of their saddles and brought them in to Darlington. The U.S. Commissioner at the agency ordered them taken to Fort Smith for trial.

Ben handcuffed his prisoners together and boarded the stage to Wichita. He anticipated no difficulty in completing the journey once the Kansas railhead was reached. But first he had to cross almost 200 miles of wild country that afforded every opportunity for delivery or escape.

The first lap of the trip was over the prairie to the Kingfisher Creek stage station below Cimarron Crossing. The prisoners indulged in threats and braggadocio in an attempt to intimidate Williams and predicted that he "wouldn't reach the Cimarron with a whole skin."

Ben at once suspected they had a confederate in the person of the keeper of the Kingfisher station. He made plans accordingly.

Before coming in sight of the station, he commanded the driver to halt the vehicle and disarmed him. Next he trussed up the prisoners so they could move neither hand or foot. The stage then proceeded to the station and drove up with the customary flourish. As the team halted, the station tender was surprised to find himself looking into the muzzle of Ben's rifle. He was relieved of his weapons.

From that moment, both tender and stage driver were on the run. The team was changed in the fastest time on record, while Ben barked orders from a point where he could cover the entire procedure. Then the vehicle shot down the bank of Kingfisher Creek and up the opposite slope in a flying getaway.

Not until reaching Cimarron Crossing several miles away was the vehicle again halted and the prisoners released from their cramped position. The Quaker marshal's audacity and fearlessness so struck them with awe that the remainder of the journey was made in silence. Both pleaded guilty to horse thievery and were sentenced to long terms at Fort Leavenworth.

Ben returned from Fort Smith with warrants for the other members of the Lee gang and orders for the military to assist in their capture. He now was received more cordially by the Cheyenne and Arapaho tribes.

Chief Little Robe sent runners out every day, and his young braves were on the scout continually. He informed the marshal that the gang had been seen on Turkey Creek near the Red

Fork Ranch headquarters.

Ben sent word to the soldiers, then set out from Little Robe's village alone. He camped one night in an old dugout at the mouth of Turkey Creek, for it was October and chilly. He had found no sign of his quarry. He decided to ride to the Red Fork headquarters where he might secure information from the ranchman.

He arose at daybreak, crossed the creek and cantered toward the log structure from the south in the early morning light. He loosened his six-shooter in its holster and shifted his Henry rifle from its saddle boot to the crook of his left arm as he searched for a chance lookout. The only sign of life was smoke issuing from the chimney. This was natural, for the ranchman would be preparing his breakfast.

With this thought, he spurred briskly around the corner of the house — straight into some fourteen ponies, saddled and tied closely together at the hitching rail! The droppings about showed they had been there all night. The prevailing silence told him he already had been seen by those inside the building.

Ben's mind raced at top speed. It was a ticklish situation. To ride away now would draw the fire of those inside.

Without hesitation, he leaped from his pony, strode to the door and kicked it open. Inside the room, with the ruffian Lee in the lead, was a full array of the men he was after standing to meet him.

His speed and daring so surprised the outlaws that they forgot to kill him the moment he came through the doorway or before he could see where to shoot. Now he had every man under his cocked rifle and swift glance.

"I can kill two or three of you if anyone opens fire!" Ben warned.

The outlaws stood like statues. All were prepared to join in the shooting the moment it started. But no one had the inclination to draw first. The marshal stood still also. He couldn't hope to arrest fourteen men single-handed.

Both sides studied the situation a full minute. Finally Lee's heavy beard broke in a snaggle-toothed grin.

"Well, here we be, Williams," he taunted. "We know you go warrants fer our arrest. Well, whyn't ye arrest us?"

Ben replied, coolly: "I'm no fool, Lee. I'll wait for a better time and place. Now that I know where you are, I'll keep on your trail until I get you — every last one!"

Without relaxing his vigilance, fixing every man with his unwavering stare, he began his retreat. The outlaws followed, a step at a time. Every man was so reluctant to let the enemy escape, and so reluctant to draw the first shot, that they unconsciously drew together until all could see out the doorway, and could be seen by the marshal outside. By the time he reached his pony, the whole gang was in the yard.

Then Ben sprang into the saddle. Keeping his drop on the crowd, he slowly backed and side-stepped his pony until the horses bunched at the rail shielded him. Then he applied the spurs. His pony shot away down the slope in a dead run, and was so far away before the gang recovered that they did not fire a shot.

Ben rode hard to the south. Within a few hours he met the cavalry detachment en route to Cimarron Crossing. He led them back to Red Fork Ranch and picked up the trail of the outlaws, now in full flight.

The second day of the pursuit they overtook and surrounded the Lee gang. The rustler chief asked for a parley and the marshal rode forward to meet him.

"I told you that I would wait for a better time

and place," Ben said. "You can submit to arrest, or I'll turn these soldiers loose on you."

The outlaws surrendered without a fight, and Ben saw them convicted and sent to join their comrades at Fort Leavenworth. Their demise also bred such wholesome respect for the Quaker marshal's nerve and resourcefulness that others of their ilk decided to leave the country.

But peace and order had not yet come for the Cheyenne and Arapaho. They had settled on their new reservation with the distinct understanding that western Indian Territory and the Texas panhandle should be the exclusive hunting grounds of the tribes of the Southern Plains. Buffalo hunters were forbidden south of the Arkansas River.

Then the Atchison, Topeka and Santa Fe railroad built up the river valley through western Kansas. It reached Dodge City in 1872, and Granada, Colorado, in 1873. By this time buffalo north of the Arkansas had become scarce, and the long-haired hide man, firing deadly, big-caliber Sharps rifles, moved into Texas and Indian Territory to gun down the Southern herd.

The government made only a token effort to keep them out. The cavalry troop from Fort Dodge spent weeks on the upper Cimarron, scouting with poor success. Dissatisfaction and unrest among the Indians grew.

Ben spent the winter among their villages, trying to console them. Although he had won the confidence of a few Cheyenne leaders and practically all the Arapaho chiefs and head men, the tribes in general were intractable. They still nursed strong feelings of vengefulness because of the injustices and wrongs they had suffered in the past. The invasion of the buffalo hunters goaded them to desperation. In the early summer of 1874, most of the Cheyenne, Comanche and part of the Kiowa tribes left their reservations on the warpath.

At dawn, June 27, 700 warriors struck the concentration of hide men at Adobe Walls, on the Canadian, in a roaring torrent of flying arrows, carbine and musket fire, wreaking such havoc and destruction that the intrepid defenders were forced to abandon the post and suspend all operations. The tribes then separated and spread across the plains, pillaging and burning.

Scattered bands scalped teamsters, cowboys and stage passengers between Kingfisher station and the Cimarron. Fifty braves under Cheyenne Chief Stone Calf attacked a wagon train near Buffalo Springs and massacred Pat Hennessey and his drivers, who were hauling supplies from Wichita to Fort Sill. Agent Miles hurried to Fort Leavenworth after soldiers for protection, and General Phil Sheridan, commanding the military department of the Southwest, launched his campaign to corral the tribes or force them into a decisive battle.

The bands of Cheyenne that remained at peace and the Arapaho, who as a tribe took no part in the war, were clustered near Darlington Agency. It was by working through them that Williams, in the closing scenes of the conflict, was able to render the outstanding service of his career.

After the Hennessey massacre, Stone Calf and his Cheyennes made their way into southwestern Kansas, where they attacked the migrant wagon of the German (often incorrectly spelled Germaine) family, killing the parents and carrying the four daughters away in captivity.

Reaching the Texas panhandle, the raiding party divided. One contingent went northwest under Chief Graybeard. Stone Calf and his followers moved southward to the Staked Plains. With Stone Calf went the two older German sisters, Catherine and Sophia. The two smaller girls, Adelaide and Julia, were hurried along afoot with Graybeard's band.

Weeks passed and the younger sisters did not know whether their older sisters were alive or dead. Graybeard wandered here and there, trying to confuse the trail, finally reaching McClellan Creek.

With soldiers pressing from all sides, the Indians became alarmed and wanted to return the two younger girls. They were pitiable objects, having been treated with utmost brutality. The squaws disliked paleface children and had forced them to work beyond their strength. Hunger and privation had reduced them to skeletons and their small hands and fingers resembled bird's claws. They were left behind, seated on a buffalo robe on a hillside, where U.S. troops under the command of Lieutenant Frank Baldwin soon found them. When the children saw the soldiers, their frenzied joy made the hardened cavalrymen turn away to hide their emotions. The girls were placed in care of Dr. J.L. Powell, assistant surgeon at Camp Supply, and taken to Fort Leavenworth.

Catherine and Sophia German were now far out on the Staked Plains. The older sisters were real prizes from the Indian way of thinking and, therefore, believed to be still alive.

Most accounts state that Colonel Nelson A. Miles of the Fifth Cavalry, who was in immediate command of the troops in the field, sent a Mexican mixed-blood from Fort Sill to the hostile camp with a secret message for the two girls telling them Julia and Adelaide were in the hands of friends. Colonel Miles also sent a formal demand for surrender to Stone Calf with the specific provision that Catherine and Sophia should be brought in alive, and Stone Calf and his followers surrendered March 1, 1875, seven miles west of Darlington.

Agency reports and Ben Williams' memoirs

show that the matter was handled somewhat differently. Every effort was being made to locate the German sisters, but the whereabouts of Stone Calf and his hostiles was utterly unknown. In this emergency an appeal was made to the Quaker marshal.

Ben saddled his pony, left behind his six-shooter and rifle, and rode to the camp of Little Robe and his less troublesome portion of the Cheyenne tribe. After establishing communication with them, he rode on to the Arapaho camp and sought out an old friend Jesse Morrison, a white man who had lived among the Indians for years and whose wife was a daughter of the Arapaho chief, Big Mouth. Big Mouth was a prominent and influential leader and had opposed the war movement from the beginning.

Morrison, Big Mouth and other Arapaho chiefs started an inquiry. Stone Calf, they determined, was south of Red River. They agreed to accompany the marshal.

It seems that Stone Calf had no knowledge of Colonel Miles' ultimatum when Ben Williams boldly walked into the camp. The Indians gave him a cool reception. However, his Arapaho companions were not slow in reminding them that "Blackbeard" was their friend like their late beloved and venerated *Tosimeah* (Agent Darlington), and that he had come to them unarmed. Stone Calf invited Ben into his tepee, where he was surprised to find the two German girls.

The girls wept with joy when they saw Williams, tears trickling down their paint-smeared faces. Stone Calf already had decided to make his way back to the vicinity of Darlington Agency, slip his people into the camp of his friend and fellow chief, Little Robe, and try to obtain the best clemency possible by voluntary surrender rather than be captured by troops off the reservation. Williams demanded custody of the white girls and offered to act as advance guard. In event soldiers were encountered, he would explain the status of his motley following. Stone Calf agreed.

The cavalcade set out for Darlington the next day, arriving at Little Robe's camp late the afternoon of March 1, without meeting a single trooper. Williams, Morrison, the Arapaho chiefs and Stone Calf then entered the office of Agent John Miles before anyone knew of their presence, or that the girls had been located.

Later, the warriors who surrendered with Stone Calf were stood in a row by Colonel Miles and the girls asked to point out those who had engaged in the murder of the other members of their family. They identified seventy-five Indians. These were sent to prison at Fort Marion, Florida.

When the war ended, Williams guided a detachment of troops into the Texas panhandle to select the site of Fort Elliott, which, like Fort Reno near Darlington, was built immediately to guard against any further outbreaks of the Plains tribes. Afterwards he continued to risk his life in the capture and delivery of criminal intruders on Cheyenne-Arapaho lands.

In 1876, government inspectors began quibbling over his salary and expenses. With Fort Reno nearly completed and an Indian police force organized under the direction of Brinton Darlington's son, Bill Darlington, Ben's services were not needed as much as before. Ben didn't argue. He resigned in disgust.

He got a job as stage driver on the Chisholm Trail between Darlington and Caldwell. On one of his trips he met and fell in love with Miss Affie Woodcock, who came down from Kansas to teach in the Indian schools. They were married a few months later.

While scouting for the Fort Elliott site in the

panhandle, Ben had discovered a splendid spring that gushed from the head of a deep ravine on Sweetwater Creek. Seven hackberry trees were scattered along the brook below the spring, and the prairie land on either side was nearly level. He never forgot the location. He told Affie about it, and persuaded her to take up a new life in the midst of the buffalo plains. Ben made a contract for purchase of the land from the government and built a house, corrals and stables.

The ranch prospered from the start. Butter, eggs and other produce were in great demand at Fort Elliott, while the herds of cattle increased. Ben maintained his friendship with the Indians, and they were often guests and always welcome at his home. His most frequent visitors was Chief Little Robe.

Ben named the place Hackberry Springs. As the country filled with settlers and a post office was established, he renamed it Affie, in honor of his wife. When Wheeler County was organized in 1879, he became one of the first county commissioners.

But Ben detested the inroads civilization was making on the plains over which he had once roamed. His neighbors were mostly Southerners, who were not averse to baiting an ex-Union soldier. His friendship with Indians galled some of them. Things reached a point where weapons might be resorted to, and Ben didn't want to kill anybody. In 1886, he sold his ranch to the S.R.E. Cattle Company and moved to California.

Here, on October 19, 1908, Ben Williams — soldier, peacemaker, frontier diplomat, scout, plainsman, ranchman, belligerent Quaker — impulsive and fearless but always fair — reached the end of his earthly journey at his home in San Jose. He was buried in a Grand Army plot in Oak Hill cemetery overlooking the restless waves of the mighty Pacific, so symbolic of his tireless

BENJAMIN F. WILLIAMS, Quaker marshal of Indian Territory, whom the Cheyenne and Arapaho called "Blackbeard."

CHEYENNE CHIEF STONE CALF with squaw.

JULIA AND ADELAIDE GERMAN, abducted by Chief Stone Calf and his Cheyennes.

and useful life.

12. Peacemaker of the Osage

Although volumes have been written on the exploits of the better-known men with silver stars and sudden guns whose ministry of law and order did much to make Indian Territory a place of opulence and good repute, as many more have been forgotten, their praises unsung.

Few have ever heard of Wiley Green Haines, peacemaker of the Osage Nation.

In the 1890s, and after the turn of the century, Haines, with only a handful of Indian police to assist him, was the lone representative of the federal government facing some of the worst riff-raff, scoundrels and criminals on earth in the sprawling, trackless wilderness which today is Oklahoma's largest county. In many cases he was also judge and jury, and sometimes executioner.

The little town of Hominy remembers him well. He reared his family there. One of the main avenues of the town bears his name, as well as additions to the city. His pearl-handled Model "P" Colt's revolver (mentioned as a rarity in John E. Parson's *The Peacemaker and Its Rivals,* William Morrow & Co., New York, 1950), still in excellent condition and kept in a bank vault by relatives, bears the inscription: "Wiley G. Haines, Hominy, O.T."

He was no "fast-draw" lawman and never had to "shoot it out at sundown." Such antics have been reserved for the fictionist and TV script writer. Old-timers describe him as a quiet man, with piercing blue eyes, shaded by a homburg-type hat. Like most officers of his day, he wore a heavy mustache, carefully trimmed. He weighed only 150 pounds, and looked much smaller than his 5 feet 7 inches in height.

It was his manner and methods that made him a giant and gained him the respect of red and white men alike. Each day threatened danger, and he thrived on it.

His first experience with law violators came when he was very young. His father, John W. Haines, a Baptist minister, and his pioneer mother lived near Santa Fe, Monroe County, Missouri, where Wiley was born October 7, 1860. The Civil War rocked the foundations of the country, and Wiley's earliest memories were the terrible scenes that followed.

Evil men roamed the state, looting and terrifying its citizens. Such a group in Monroe County called themselves the "Home Guard." The honest inhabitants organized to protest their activities. The Home Guard axed off the head of one of its members and swore that the "Protestors" had killed him. Thirty men, including Wiley's father, were seized by the rebels and marched off to prison.

Ten died before a firing squad. Most of the others died from maltreatment. John Haines managed to escape. But before he could rejoin his family, two scalawags came to the house, covered his wife with pistols and demanded her money.

Mrs. Haines defied them, so they told her, "We will kill you."

The courageous woman stood her ground. "If men are so low as to murder helpless women for a little money, I would rather not live," she said.

"All right," threatened the outlaws, "we'll take your son."

"You'll have to kill me too!" little Wiley shouted, emerging from behind his mother's skirts. He was barely able to hold the double-barreled shotgun pointed at the men's bellies, but his small finger was on the trigger.

The cowed pair rode off without loot.

John Haines finally reached home. Strain and worry had taken its toll of his wife's health. He started west with his family in search of more favorable climes.

Mrs. Haines died on the way. Her death and reports of Indian raids on the Kansas plains caused John Haines to turn back to Missouri. At age thirteen, Wiley managed their new farm in Lawrence County while his father continued preaching.

John Haines wanted his son to become a minister, but the western frontier was the greater attraction. In 1878, Wiley joined some other young adventurers and successfully drove a herd of cattle from Cedar County through the Indian ravaged southwest to the Rio Verde region near Prescott, Arizona.

Describing the trek in later years, he wrote:

> I might have been that freckle-faced pioneer lad in Emerson Hough's famous novel, *The Covered Wagon* . . . . We were on the trail 137 days. Before starting the drive, I bought my first six-shooter and a rifle, and I learned to use both with accuracy.
>
> I arrived in Arizona with five cents in my pocket and a great determination. For two years I worked as a cowboy, but wanted something in life whereby I could better serve humanity. In 1880, I joined a caravan of wagons heading back east. Our progress was threatened by the presence of the Apache, Victorio, who was terrorizing the district. However, extra precautions were taken, fortifications were built around each camp, and Victorio and his band never appeared. Just 100 days later, the train arrived safely in Missouri.

224

Wiley went to Bolivar, where his father had become superintendent of the Southwest Baptist College. He completed his education there, and for a short time taught school in Cedar County. In 1887, he went to California at the behest of a doctor uncle to study medicine, and might have made the Pacific Coast his home, "except that the western movement was still in his blood."

New frontiers were being carved from Indian Territory. The glowing pictures being painted by the press of this vast region fascinated him, and when the Unassigned Lands were opened to settlement on April 22, 1889, Wiley rode the first train into Oklahoma City.

Real estate was the booming business. He entered this profession first and married Sarah E. Tapp, the daughter of a friendly associate, from Illinois. In 1890, when Oklahoma was organized as a separate territory with seven counties and the territorial governor appointed Captain C.H. DeFord first sheriff at Oklahoma City, DeFord gave Wiley the job of guarding his prisoners. This began his career in law enforcement.

Charles F. Colcord, who succeeded DeFord as sheriff in the first territorial elections, promoted Wiley to criminal deputy, and he helped bring in many of the county's first badmen. In 1893, when the Cherokee Outlet was opened to settlement and more counties were formed, Wiley went to Perry to become a deputy under Sheriff J.C. Scruggs of Noble County. Bill Tilghman was city marshal and Heck Thomas his assistant, and Wiley worked with these famed lawmen several months taming Perry's turbulent section called "Hell's Half Acre."

Persons committing crimes in the territorial counties often fled into the adjoining Indian Nations and reservations, and sheriffs and their deputies had no authority to pursue them across these borders. The Organic Act of 1890 had given the United States Marshal at Guthrie concurrent jurisdiction with sheriffs in all criminal matters, so a number of local officers were issued federal commissions.

Wiley carried such a commission. As a federal officer, he made many trips from Perry after bad-men into the Osage country.

It was a land of blackjack forests, towering bluffs and yawning canyons, and a haven for such notorious gangs as the Cooks, Daltons, Doolins and the Starrs. It was almost impossible to apprehend a fugitive in the section. The only law was the Indian agency police force operating under the Department of the Interior. But Haines became so uncannily successful in entering this junglelike wilderness and returning with his man and a whole skin that, in June 1898, he was appointed constable for the Indian service and stationed at Hominy (then Hominy Post), thirty miles south of Pawhuska.

To this little scattering of cabins along Hominy Creek, Haines brought his wife and three children, John, Wiley Jr., and Mary. Few white families lived at the post. Schools and roads were non-existent. But wild game was plentiful and Haines brought a few cattle to fatten on the lush bluestem. So the family fared well. Six other children were born at Hominy: Rhalls, Virgil, Warren, Robert, Ironica and Elma.

Haines had obtained his appointment through civil service, and the Indian Agent Colonel J.W. Pollock felt offended. When Haines presented his credentials at Pawhuska, Pollock handed him his first assignment.

"If you are so good," Pollock said, "go out and eject Henry Behining." Behining was a white man reputed to be dangerous. He had refused to pay a monthly fee to do business on the reservation. Haines rode out to see him. Behining met him with a cocked revolver.

"I can kill you easily," Behining said.

"You could," Haines replied, calmly, "but you couldn't kill the law."

"I can whip hell out of you with my bare fists," the man snarled, still pointing his revolver at Haines' forehead.

Haines knew the crisis had passed.

"You wouldn't want to whip a man you held no grudge against. Now, just to have it said you weren't guilty of a damn fool trick like assaulting a federal officer, put up that gun."

Cursing, Behining holstered his weapon. Haines took him to Pawhuska, and the next day escorted Behining off the reservation. "Henry returned later to become Osage County's first engineer," Haines recalled. "We were always the best of friends."

Agent Pollock's attitude changed also. In less than a month he offered Haines' services to the War Department to go to the Philippines to capture the islands' worst outlaw, Emilio Aguinaldo.

The United States had been wrestling its first colonial problem since the end of the war with Spain. The Filipinos had expected independence. Instead, the islands had been annexed by the United States. Many of the "liberated" people disliked American rule, and two days before the Senate ratified the annexation treaty, Filipino insurgents attacked the American expeditionary forces at Manila. Aguinaldo had become the guiding spirit of the insurrection.

In fight after fight the Americans beat back the poorly equipped rebel army. Realizing they could not win by conventional warfare, the Filipinos resorted to guerrilla tactics for which the harassed Americans were totally unprepared. Aguinaldo proclaimed himself president of the Philippine Republic. A veteran of revolutionary activity, he seemed to possess a mystical power to resist bullets and capture. Intelligence officers had been unable to discover his whereabouts and knew only that the rebel army commanders received orders from a secret headquarters somewhere on Luzon Island.

"If he's on Luzon, Haines can find him, single-handed and within sixty days," Pollock declared. "If he fails to do so, I will personally pay all expenses."

The War Department declined the offer. They sent, instead, a tough little army officer named Frederick Funston. It was not until eighteen months later, however, that Funston, with his 20th Kansas regiment, was able to locate and destroy the rebel headquarters at Palanan, in the northern mountains of Luzon, capture Aguinaldo and end the rebellion.

Funston's daring exploit was the talk of America in the spring of 1901. But Pollock maintained, "Haines could have shortened the fighting by at least a year."

He moved Haines to Pawhuska and promoted him assistant to Chief of the Indian Police Warren Bennett. Bennett was only thirty-five, and a vigorous, popular officer. But as more areas of Oklahoma were opened to settlers and more fugitives sought sanctuary in the reservation, he had been forced to spread his forces too thinly. He welcomed Haines and gave him free reign to use whatever methods he deemed necessary.

The country teemed with horse thieves and whiskey peddlers. The Indians and honest whites not in sympathy with such activities were hesitant to cooperate. When Haines launched his campaign, he received anonymous threats against his life.

Late one afternoon he left Pawhuska in a buggy on one of his regular visits to his family. As he crossed Bird Creek, a rifle cracked without warning above the trail and a bullet whizzed past his head.

He grabbed his Winchester from the seat, sprang to the ground and ran quickly to where smoke still hung over some boulders. He shouted to his foe, challenging him to fire again. But the would-be assassin had vanished. It was dark before Haines gave up the search and drove on to Hominy.

He kept a daily journal of his expeditions, in which he described one typical clash as follows:

Feb. 4. Am notified that thieves again made a raid on Indian horses. I go north of Hominy ½ mi. & strike their trail & discover their camp after having ridden 35 miles. I advance afoot. I observe several objects through (the) brush of a blackjack tree. I call, "You, there, hold up your hands!" I see a scramble for guns but no sign of obeyance to order. I fire & advance 2 or 3 steps. Call again, "Hold up your hands!" Am not obeyed. I fire again & advance & find that I have fatally shot two horse thieves named Myers and Brooksher . . . .

Feb. 5. Take bodies of parties killed yesterday to Agency.

Besides stock thieves, whiskey runners and fugitives from justice, he had to contend with unscrupulous whites who came to trade with the Indians, exploit their lands and cheat them at cards. Haines' eye and arm was quicker than the most rapid action of the best pistol-toters. Usually the ready revolver was snatched from their grasp and sent flying.

With ruffians who boasted of their physical prowess it was the same story. He bumped heads together and lugged them off to jail. In extreme cases, they went to the hospital first. He drove the tough outsiders from the reservation, and even the quarrelsome mixed-breeds, often a source of annoyance and danger, became quiet and subdued.

Department of the Interior officials gloried in Haines, not so much for his handy gun and fists, but because he maintained order at a minimum of expense and his integrity was unquestioned. He once guarded, alone, a $125,000 payment to the Osage Indians. By a quirk in the law, he could have stolen the money, hidden it, and if the theft was proven, would have had to spend only one year in federal prison.

He is remembered best, however, for his pitched battle with the murdering Martin brothers on a sweltering August afternoon in 1903 . . . .

Sam and Will Martin, "two hell-raising farm boys," had been a constant source of trouble around Mulhall, a small Logan County community north of Guthrie. In the spring of 1899 they shot up the town, causing a neighbor's team to run away, wrecking his wagon. The neighbor, C.M. Hull, filed charges in justice court, but local authorities failed to act, and Sam Martin promised: "We'll square accounts with you, Hull — sooner or later!"

The evening of May 22, Hull left Mulhall in a buggy. At a point where the road took a sudden turn upward to his prairie homestead, the Martins rode in on either side, covering him with revolvers.

Sam, 24, a slouch hat pulled low over his shaggy head and a quid of tobacco bulging his bearded jaw, informed him: "This is a stick-up."

"I have $10," Hull said. "It's in my right pocket."

"Ten dollars!" Will, three years younger than his brother, with a pointed chin and nervous tic

230

under his left eye, showed his yellowed teeth in a grin. "You're gonna need more'n that—"

"Shut up, Will," Sam cut in. He took Hull's purse. The hate in his eyes was tempered only by his soft drawl. "You can do one of two things, mister. You can get out of the country, or deliver us $500 on this spot by noon tomorrow."

Hull was stupefied. "I don't have that kind of money. I would have to sell my farm — everything I own."

"Raise it anyway you like," Sam said, "or we'll dynamite your house while you're asleep — we'll burn your barn down."

Hull drove home and sat up the rest of the night discussing the threat with his wife. He decided to increase the mortgage on his farm. But next morning, his Mulhall banker told him, "You're already mortgaged too heavily."

When Hull explained his problem, the banker advised him to have the Martins arrested.

"I've tried that," Hull replied, "but our officers wouldn't go after them."

"Then," said the banker, "you had better go to Guthrie and talk to the county attorney."

At Guthrie, an extortion complaint was prepared but Hull was too frightened to sign it. So County Attorney Edgar W. Jones issued an information writ, endorsed Hull as prosecuting witness, and ordered Sheriff Frank Rinehart to serve it. Two of Rinehart's deputies, Charley Carpenter and Joe Reynolds, crawled into a spring wagon and rattled north across the Cimarron to make the arrests.

The Martins were not at home but a neighbor had seen them riding past with Clarence Simmons, a young farmer friend who lived a few miles further west. The officers drove to the Simmons place.

The two-story frame house stood on a high hill that sloped toward a creek. A brush-choked draw ran behind past the barn to the southwest and the low ground between was covered by a heavy thicket. There were no horses in sight, no sign of life.

Reynolds waited beside the wagon while Carpenter, Winchester in hand, stepped to the door and knocked. Simmons came to the door.

"We hold warrants for the Martins," Carpenter said. "We understand they are here."

Simmons didn't answer, but glanced toward the barn. The deputy waited expectantly. Simmons remained inscrutable.

"They in the barn?" Carpenter demanded. "Speak up, or we'll arrest you too—"

He heard rustling inside as two persons came down the stairs. A moment later, the back door slammed. Carpenter levered a cartridge into his rifle, Reynolds grabbed his shotgun from the wagon, and they ran around opposite sides of the house. Reynolds reached his corner first. He saw the Martins racing for the draw.

"Hold up, boys!" he yelled.

Sam dropped to one knee and fired with his Colt's. Will ducked behind a couple of small trees and opened fire with his six-shooter. Reynolds cut down on him with the shotgun. Will fell forward between the trees.

Carpenter was using his rifle industriously on Sam. Sam staggered, went to his knees, but was up again in a second and disappeared in the brush. Carpenter pursued him. By the time he reached the draw, Sam had mounted his horse and vanished.

Carpenter discovered Will's horse tied in the thicket and rode back to the wounded outlaw. Will was bleeding badly from the chest and neck. Simmons helped the officers load the outlaw into the wagon and haul him to Guthrie and a doctor.

Sheriff Rinehart and his deputies kept a strict

vigil at the Simmons and Martin farms and furnished Hull and his wife protection. But Sam apparently had left the country.

Much to the chagrin of everybody, the grand jury failed to indict Will, and he was released. With a few days he, too, disappeared. Somewhere he rejoined Sam. When next heard from the Martins were well on their way to eclipse anything accomplished by the Cooks, Daltons, Doolins and Starrs.

On July 2, they robbed the store and post office at Hopeton, Woods County, and fled into Kansas. During the next several months a dozen stores in western Kansas were robbed and one settler slain as they continued northwest, posing as drifting cowboys.

Reaching Colorado, they teamed up with a desperado named "Indian Bill" Smith. On November 28, 1902, the trio held up the post office at Carlton. Sam and Will escaped, but a postal clerk recognized Indian Bill. Smith was arrested by Undersheriff J.H. Frisbie, of Prowers County, tried at Pueblo and sentenced to five years at Leavenworth. The government offered rewards for the Martins.

During the next few months they were reported seen in No Man's Land, the Texas panhandle, and as far away as Albuquerque, New Mexico. By the spring of 1903, they were back in Oklahoma.

On March 2, they held up the Rock Island railroad depot at Hennessey and killed an innocent bystander, Gus Cravett. Sheriffs, federal marshals and citizen posses combed the western half of the territory without apprehending them. At 4 o'clock the morning of July 8, they appeared at Geary, Blaine County, shot and killed City Marshal John Cross, took his badge and silver watch as souvenirs, and vanished again. Rewards for their capture, dead or alive, totaled $12,000 . . . .

233

Wiley Haines received copies of the reward notices at Pawhuska. He memorized their descriptions and obtained a photograph of Will Martin taken in the Guthrie jail. On July 14, he learned that the brothers had entered the Osage.

At 2 o'clock on this Sunday afternoon, a citizen named Fred Keeler drove along the main road from Pawhuska toward Bartlesville in his buggy. He was halted by Sam Martin, searched and taken to a secluded spot off the highway and guarded by Will. A few minutes later, Dave Ware, a retired peace officer of considerable reputation, drove past and received the same treatment. Ware, unarmed, gnashed his teeth in helpless anger.

For hours the holdups continued. No passerby escaped. By 6 P.M., more than a hundred men and women were herded together, bandying jokes with the robbers. Ware was the particular target of Sam Martin.

"Ware, you're a killer," he said. "Why don't you do something?"

"To hell with you," rejoined Ware. "You've got the drop now . . . ."

From 55 head of horses, the Martins chose three of the best animals and saddles. At nightfall, they released the prisoners and disappeared.

It was the most startling piece of banditry in the annals of frontier crime.

Haines scouted the area but found no trace of the fugitives. Bounty hunters from all over Oklahoma and Indian territories and as far away as Fort Worth and Kansas City hurried into the region. For three weeks they filtered through the wilderness.

Haines waited.

In the hills southwest of Pawhuska a band of Osages camped on Bird Creek. At noon, August 3, a white man came down to the stream near their tepees for water. They noted that he wore two six-shooters on well-filled cartridge belts and carried a rifle.

As he disappeared over the hill, an Indian trailed him silently. The Indian rode eight miles that afternoon to Haines' office in Pawhuska. Two strangers were camped below Wooster Mound, he said. Wiley knew who those strangers were.

Quietly he passed the word to Chief Bennett and Indian policeman Henry Majors. The three officers mounted and rode from town into the lowering sun, slowly. Their quarry could best be surprised at dusk.

They left their mounts behind the last ridge and edged closer on foot. The camp lay in a deep ravine beyond the knoll. Three horses stood tied in the timber. Nearby, Sam and Will Martin rested behind a pile of saddles.

The officers separated. Majors took the left rim of the ravine. Bennett took the right flank. Wiley moved into the face of the camp.

As he darted across the opening to a fallen tree, one of the horses snorted. Sam, then Will, leaped from behind the saddle heap, rifles in hand.

There was no time for his companions to reach position. Wiley drew a quick bead and fired. Will Martin dropped from sight. Sam dashed for the horses. Wiley fired again and saw the outlaw twist half around, triggering a wild shot as he fell.

Bennett abandoned his course and ran to Wiley's side. Majors held his position on the rim, covering them. The two officers charged the outlaw behind the saddles.

Will Martin was dead. Haines' bullet had struck him in the mouth, tearing away the back of his head. Sam lay in the shadows where he had fallen, rifle clutched under his body.

"I think you got him too," Bennett said.

Wiley drew his pearl-handled revolver — a more effective weapon at close range — and moved forward to investigate. He saw Sam Martin's hand jerk, and leaped sideways. The outlaw's soft-nosed rifle bullet struck Haines high inside the right shoulder, the lead and its copper jacket bursting into a hundred fragments. Particles of the metal were driven into the officer's lungs, rupturing innumerable small blood vessels.

The impact knocked the six-shooter from his hand and he fell, an open target for the tricky killer. Sam Martin, though mortally wounded, still had the strength to trigger a final shot. But Bennett, leaping past Haines, was on him in a second, kicking the rifle from his grasp and threatening to blow out his brains.

The Indians in camp heard the shooting and came over the hill. They helped carry the wounded officer and the two outlaws to Pawhuska.

Bennett and Majors brought in the plunder — two rifles, four revolvers, a half-dozen latest style cartridge belts, nearly 1000 rounds of ammunition, and the horses and saddles stolen in the holdups on the road to Bartlesville.

In Will Martin's pockets they found the badge and silver watch belonging to the slain marshal of Geary.

Sam Martin died that night, boasting of his many crimes: "I've robbed more people than any man in history. Why, in one afternoon, I robbed more'n a hundred . . . ." But just before he expired, he admitted: "Reckon I've been on the wrong trail."

It was a long time before Haines recovered from his wounds. He received letters and telegrams from throughout the territory, scores of friends called personally to congratulate him, and the United States district attorney at

Guthrie sent his written commendation.

The myth that the trackless Osage Nation was a safe place to hide had been exploded in the gunsmoke at Wooster Mound.

Haines had years of law enforcement ahead of him. A few days after he left the hospital, he captured Walter McLain, one of the last of thirteen prisoners who, seven years previous, had escaped with the notorious Bill Doolin from the Guthrie federal jail. Doolin had been slain at Lawson, on the Payne-Pawnee county line, by Deputy Marshal Heck Thomas.

In 1905, Warren Bennett died from an unexpected, severe hemorrhage of the lungs, and Haines succeeded him as Chief of the Osage Police. With statehood in 1907, the Indian police system was abolished, and until 1915, Haines served as officer for the Department of the Interior and deputy sheriff. During 1927, he played a prominent role as special investigator for Governor Henry S. Johnston in suppressing liquor traffic in northeastern Oklahoma.

He was now 68. His children were grown. He had seen Indian villages become thriving cities. He had witnessed the oil booms that made the Osages the wealthiest people per capita on earth. And he had seen the ghost towns that remained. But he kept a furious pace.

In 1928, he filed as Democratic candidate for sheriff of Osage County. That he conducted a vigorous campaign is evidenced by his posters, which read:

No Snitches Will Be Tolerated. I Think A Snitch Is A Copperhead Snake, He Will Bite You If He Can.

The afternoon of September 23, he ascended the courthouse steps to greet some old friends. While talking to them, he slumped into the arms

237

WILEY GREEN HAINES, "Peacemaker of the Osage."

WARREN BENNETT, Chief of the Osage Police.

239

ARSENAL OF Martin brothers and stolen horses recovered following gun battle at Wooster Mound. Inserts: Will Martin (left) and Sam Martin (right) in death.

WILEY G. HAINES

DEMOCRATIC CANDIDATE

For SHERIFF

Osage County

PRIMARY ELECTION, AUGUST 7

No Snitches Will Be Tolerated

I THINK A SNITCH IS A COPPERHEAD SNAKE, HE WILL BITE YOU IF HE CAN

CAMPAIGN POSTER of Wiley Haines as Democratic candidate for sheriff of Osage County.

241

of Deputy Sheriff Ed Clewien and breathed his last.

He was buried in the Hominy city cemetery. His wife Sarah lies beside him. A lone pine, symbolic of his life, shades the flat, rectangular stone. The single clue to his strength and character can be read in his simple epitaph: "An Honest Man Is the Noblest Work of God."

13. "Carry Nation" Lawman

Engineer Joseph Hotchkiss realized what was happening the moment he saw the light change from green to red at Blackstone switch, near Wybark, eight miles north of Muskogee, Creek Nation. It was 9:57 o'clock the moon-bright night of November 13, 1894 — the year that trains on the M.K.&T. and Iron Mountain railroad running through Indian Territory were constantly being held up and their express and baggage cars looted. Someone had opened the switch. Instead of going on down the main line, the northbound Katy No. 2 shot onto the side track. Hotchkiss set his brakes, opened the sand valves and brought the train to a grinding, screeching halt.

Obviously he had stopped the train sooner than the outlaws expected. Four robbers — Nathaniel Reed, alias "Texas Jack," Tom Root, a dangerous Cherokee, and Buz Luckey and Will Smith, Negroes — dashed onto the tracks and ran toward the engine, shooting and yelling. Reed had been "tipped" by a contact in Dallas that the northbound Katy was carrying a shipment of $60,000. His plan was to stop the train on the siding and blast open the express car with dynamite.

What Reed hadn't been told was that American Express Company officials had just instituted a new policy of placing armed guards on all shipments running through the Indian country.

Inside the express car with two crackshot assistants, Paden Tolbert and Sid Johnson, was veteran lawman "Bud" Ledbetter, whose exploits on the Indian frontier were to become legendary.

As the robbers rushed the train, Hotchkiss jumped from the engine cab and hid in a small ravine. Then Ledbetter, icy blue eyes snapping, his dark brown handlebar mustache bristling and 220 pounds of hard muscle tensed for action, ordered both large side doors of the express car opened. A guard appeared in each of these, throwing lead as fast as they could lever their Winchesters, and drove the outlaws back.

Reed and his gang had nerve. They took positions behind trees on each side of the train. For nearly an hour they fired into the wooden coaches, allowing no one to leave, and after numerous threats finally hurled a charge of dynamite that blew off the end of the express car. But Ledbetter and his men stuck to their posts and kept using their rifles.

During the battle, Texas Jack slipped under cover of some cross-ties stacked along the tracks and entered the front of the first passenger coach, wearing false whiskers and carrying a gunnysack. While the firing was still hot outside, he passed through the entire train. As he entered each coach, he shouted, "Everybody drop his valuables in this sack or be killed!" He collected $460, eight watches and three pistols, even forcing one young passenger to go with him and hold one side of the sack.

Things went well until he was leaving the last coach. Ledbetter, through the ragged aperture of splintered boards of the express car, had only a brief glimpse of him. It was all Bud needed. His Winchester roared. Jack fell, badly wounded in the kidneys and hip. He managed to drag himself to the shelter of the cross-ties. Buz Luckey, a big, strong man, picked him up and carried him to his horse. Texas Jack had enough, and he gave the order to retreat. After a few more shots, Smith and Root rushed to their horses, and all fled into the night. Engineer Hotchkiss crawled from hiding, backed the train onto the main line and proceeded to Gibson station to await orders.

Reed clung to his mount a distance of about two miles. Unable to bear the pain any longer, he divided the loot with his companions, and they left him wrapped in a blanket under a ledge of rock. Later, they took him into the woods to the home of a hog thief named Dick Reynolds to be cared for. From there, he made his way to Seneca, Missouri, and a few weeks later, reached his brother's home in the Boston Mountains of Arkansas.

At daybreak Ledbetter and his guards were back to pick up the robbers' trail. They found bloodstains under the rock where Reed had rested and traced him to Reynolds' house. An Indian woman told them the outlaws had been there and gone.

American Express Company officials in Chicago lauded Ledbetter and his men for "a valiant stand against these desperadoes in defense of the property in their charge," and offered a $250 reward for each robber captured and convicted. At Fort Smith, United States Marshal George Crump sent a large force of deputies into the field, and at Muskogee, the peppery U.S. marshal for the Northern District of Indian Territory, S. Morton Rutherford, spearheaded a thorough search in the Creek Nation. By this time, they knew the identity of the men they were after.

Buz Luckey was the first captured. He was jailed at Fort Smith and given fifteen years in prison. Tom Root was shot and killed near Concharty, Will Smith left the country never to be seen again, and Texas Jack surrendered to federal officers in Arkansas. Jack received a five-year sentence, and a parole one year later. He became an evangelist, traveling with Wild West acts and lecturing on crime-does-not-pay until his death from old age at Tulsa, Oklahoma, January 7, 1950.

Nathaniel Reed was the first, but he wasn't the last Indian Territory desperado into whom Ledbetter's bullets put the fear of God. But that's getting ahead of our story .... To best understand our hero is to understand the volcanic society of the 1880s and 1890s into which he strode by virtue of his incredible judgment and coolness, wielding a Colt's six-shooter and Winchester rifle with which he could shoot the lobe off a man's ear and never put a mark on his jaw.

James Franklin Ledbetter was born "in a log cabin somewhere on War Eagle Creek" in Madison County, Arkansas, December 15, 1852. His father also was named James, and for a time he was called "Little Jimmie." When that no longer seemed appropriate because of his six-foot-two inch frame, they called him "Bud." In 1874, he married Mary Josephine Terry, a Missouri girl. A son George W. was born to the couple August 28, 1875, followed by a daughter, America Jane "Dolly," in 1877. During this period, Bud moved his little family near Coal Hill, in Johnson County.

One afternoon he came into town to stock up on supplies and strolled into one of the many saloons in this boisterous, booming mining settlement. A group of town bullies, a little high on raw whiskey, happened to be gathered there.

Bud, on this summer day, was wearing a white linen suit, and the unusual garb attracted the attention of the roughly dressed loungers. Their sense of judgment dulled by alcohol, they failed to take into account the stature of the stranger. They immediately gathered around him, finger-ing and tugging at his suit "to test the material." One tough jerked Ledbetter's shirt tail out "to see if it was real silk."

Bud's eyes chilled. Without a word he walked out of the saloon, followed by jeers from the group. He went down the street to a hardware store and purchased a hefty new oaken axe handle. Then he returned to the saloon and closed and locked the door behind him.

Passersby heard the commotion. Unable to gain entrance, they hastily summoned the town mayor. This official, with the help of several citizens, forced open the door. They pushed inside and saw half a dozen saloon habitues scattered over the pine floor, unconscious. Ledbetter leaned on the bar, tapping the heavy axe handle across the palm of his big left hand, cold eyes boring the mayor, and asking, "What are you going to do about it?"

The mayor, momentarily disconcerted, didn't reply. Finally he turned to the crowd and said: "Clear these bums out of here, then we'll get to the bottom of this."

"Getting to the bottom" of the affair amounted to the town fathers insisting that Ledbetter accept the job of town marshal. It was the beginning of a fantastic career that would bring him to Indian Territory.

He was appalled at the dangerous conditions as Coal Hill's responsible citizens. The town was a fertile place for gunplay. Bud had plenty of experience with a rifle from his boyhood days hunting along War Eagle Creek and could smash a whiskey glass on a post at twenty paces with a six-shooter simply by pointing the weapon. In most cases he had only to "club" the violator off to confinement. Such deeds required plenty of muscle and raw courage; it was a language the miners understood and respected.

At the same time, he launched a campaign

against the more vice-ridden drinking halls and sin-dens. Acting on legal warrants and injunctions, he padlocked them one by one. But Bud was a fair, reasonable man. These hotspots provided what the miners considered wholesome recreation, and those who agreed to strict supervision were allowed to re-open.

Within a week, it was safe for a peace loving fellow to step into a saloon for a quick drink without being messed up or rawhided.

Bud's enforcement methods attracted the attention of some of Arkansas' best known peace officers. Sheriff E.T. McConnell, fiery disciple of law and order at Clarksville, rode over to Coal Hill.

He told Bud: "Anybody who can tame this burg belongs on my force. How'd you like to be my deputy at double the money you're getting now?"

The proposal surprised Bud, but he accepted. A month later he became deputy sheriff of Johnson County and served fourteen years, helping clear the section of its murderers and thieves. It was during this period that he also established his reputation for dogged pursuit. He trailed one killer and jail-breaker named Holland four weeks on horseback from Johnson County to Blanton, Tennessee — a distance of 1,000 miles!

Little wonder then, in 1894, that the American Express Company, seeking reliable men to guard their huge shipments through the Indian Nations, decided no man had more nerve or could fill the position better than Bud Ledbetter of Clarksville.

Bud went to Muskogee and started work July 27. After riding up and down the line half a dozen times without any excitement, he threatened to quit. The company assured him that "hell usually popped when it was least expected," and, of course, the train crews were constantly talking about what they would do in case another holdup occurred.

Bud asked Hotchkiss what he would do if the robbers got into his cab and ordered him to stop.

The engineer replied: "Well, I'd just knock 'em in the head with my hammer and keep the train moving."

However, when he saw Texas Jack and his boys running toward the train, this brave soul had forgotten his hammer completely and dashed for cover.

After the Blackstone switch outlaws had been rounded up, things became slack in the holdup business. Ledbetter worked for the express company only a few more months. He wanted a job with more action. He thought of returning to Clarksville, but his services were needed in the Nations.

In 1889 Congress had established the first white man's court in Indian Territory at Muskogee. Principally a court for civil matters, it was given exclusive original jurisdiction over all offenses against the laws of the United States not punishable by death or imprisonment at hard labor. Such cases still went to the federal court for the Western District of Arkansas.

Since the Civil War, fugitives from all parts of the country had found Indian Territory an ideal place for hiding and continuing their depredations. Outlaw gangs rode pell-mell through the settlements, pistols spouting lead. They ransacked stores, robbed and killed lone travelers, stole horses and cattle, and made forays on banks in the border towns of Arkansas, Texas and Missouri.

There were 64,000 square miles to roam over, from Red River to Kansas and west to the Texas panhandle and No Man's Land, and 70,000 people, patroled by only 200 United States deputy marshals from Judge Parker's court at Fort

Smith. Many of those captured had died on the court's infamous gallows, and the marshals were quick on the draw and slow to scare. But this did not mean that they always came out winners. More than fifty were slain in the line of duty. Some were surprised and murdered and left on the prairies or in canyons in unmarked graves.

The pressure was somewhat alleviated with the opening of the western half of the Indian country to settlement by the "runs" of 1889 through 1893, and the organization of this section as the Territory of Oklahoma. Finally, on March 1, 1895, Congress divided the remaining area of the Five Civilized Tribes into three judicial districts — Northern, covering the seven small tribes of the Quapaw Agency and the area of the Creek and Cherokee nations, with headquarters at Muskogee; the Central district, embracing the Choctaw Nation, with headquarters at McAlester, and the Southern district, comprising Seminole and Chickasaw nations, with headquarters at Ardmore.

In this new set-up Ledbetter saw opportunity for the action desired. On June 25, 1895, he was appointed United States deputy marshal for the Northern district under S. Morton Rutherford.

He scarcely had finished polishing his badge when a bad Cherokee named Big Jim McAlford went on a rampage down in the old Belle Starr country on the Canadian River west of Porum. McAlford murdered one of his neighbors, set fire to the house with the body inside, and was running wild about the terror-stricken countryside, everyone afraid to arrest him.

The U.S. district attorney handed Bud the warrant. Marshal Rutherford suggested that he take a posse to bring in such a depraved killer. Bud insisted on going alone, saying: "McAlford's a coward at heart — he wouldn't shoot a man so long as he was walking toward him."

His prediction proved true. Big Jim was noted for his physical prowess, but when Bud informed him that he carried federal papers and would kill him if necessary, he surrendered without a fight. Ledbetter took him to Muskogee in leg irons "to be sure he didn't slip anything over on him."

He was given a preliminary hearing, released on bond, and returned to Porum. A few days before his trial, he and two friends started for Muskogee in a spring wagon — all three in the front seat with Big Jim in the middle. They had gone about five miles when a bullet came whining from a clump of bushes at the roadside and struck McAlford in the neck, killing him instantly. His companions, believing they were next, whipped the team into a hard run and never looked back. But no other shots were fired. The assassin apparently had got the man he was after. McAlford's body was returned to Porum, and no one ever knew who killed him.

Everyone in the district looked forward to the annual stomp dance that was held during the latter part of August in the bottoms between Hominy and Bird creeks north of Tulsa. Indians came from as far away as Shawnee, Tecumseh and Wewoka, the young bucks on horseback and the old men and women and children in two-seated hacks or light wagons. They brought their tepees, bedding, all their dogs, dance costumes and medicine bag. Beeves were killed and distributed to each tepee. What the Indians didn't eat, the dogs and flies carried off. Dances, in which three to five-hundred Indians took part to the beat of tom-toms and rattle of turtle shells, continued throughout the night. Many whites also attended the affair and a platform was erected on which they performed old time square dances.

Ledbetter, with deputy marshals Frank Jones and Bea Mellon, filtered through the crowds, trying to keep order and watching for bootleggers selling whiskey to the Indians. In spite of them there were several fights and much drinking.

Frank Sennett, Alec Daniels and Henry Childers, enemies for years, met on the grounds and renewed their quarrel. Sennett beat Daniels to the draw, killed him. Lon Cannady, a friend of Daniels, then shot Sennett. Two men lay dead before Ledbetter and the other deputies reached the scene, and Henry Childers was looking for Cannady.

Bea Mellon tried to arrest him to stop the fighting, and Henry jumped on his horse, making a wild dash through the crowd. Indians and whites scattered every direction to escape injury. Mellon yelled for him to halt, but Henry kept putting the spurs to his horse. Mellon cut down on him with his Winchester. Henry fell from the saddle, dead.

Sam Childers, Henry's brother, was there and had plenty of nerve. It was soon whispered around that he was getting some of the boys together and there would be more bloodshed. Ledbetter, knowing the consequences of such a battle, called Sam to one side and told him:

"Start anything like that and you are the first one I will kill. The best thing for you to do is take Henry's body to town and forget the whole matter."

Sam decided to take Bud's advice.

One of the most notorious gangs in Indian Territory was the Turner brothers and two Turkey Track cowboys, Bob Cloud and Jim Pendleton. They stayed in the hills south of the Cimarron on the western border of the Creek Nation, and would go over into Oklahoma, rob stores and settlers, then hide out at the Jane Wolf ranch on Salt Creek. Marshal Rutherford assigned Ledbetter and Frank Jones to bring them in.

While Bud and Frank were making plans for

the expedition they ran into Austin Bell, whom Jones had known while foreman on a ranch in Texas. Bell was always on the scout and at the time wanted for a crime recently committed. Bud and Frank promised to do what they could to help him out of his trouble if he would line up with them. Bell agreed and went to the Jane Wolf ranch where he joined forces with the Turners and left with them on one of their trips to Oklahoma.

Bud and Frank made camp on Salt Creek, some distance from the ranch, fought mosquitoes big as horseflies day and night, and waited. On the seventh day, their patience worn thin, they decided to relax and do some fishing. It wasn't long until they had a big string of black bass.

That evening, when Frank had fried the fish crisp and golden brown and Bud's dutch oven bread was almost done, the bushes parted and out stepped Bell. He reported that the outlaws had just ridden in. They were in the ranch house, all well armed and drinking heavily.

That was all Bud and Frank wanted to know. Grabbing their Winchesters, they slipped up to the ranch in the darkness. The house was a double log affair with an entry way between the wings. Frank went in the back door and Bud in the front. A few minutes later when they met in the entry way each had two prisoners, handcuffed.

They were soon ready to begin their trip to Muskogee, but first had to go by camp for their outfit. And this was the tragic part of the story. When they arrived they found their fish truly were black bass. In the excitement they had forgotten to take them off the fire. For years afterwards there were many arguments among old-timers whether the capture of the Turner gang was really worth giving up that skillet full of fish. Bud got Austin Bell's case dismissed in Texas. But it wasn't the last time he used an informer to bring outlaws to justice.

Old Man Green, an intermarried Cherokee, had a small farm on the Caney River west of Oologah. Two of his boys, Bill and Ed, worked on the Mashed-O Ranch and were top cowhands until Milt Barker hired them to kill a Shawnee Indian named George Walden.

Walden lived in a tent on Buck Creek, north of Tulsa. He and Barker had traded wives. After the trade, Walden learned that his former wife was due some money from the sale of land and demanded the wives be swapped back. Barker figured he was entitled to the money and offered to split it with the Green boys if they would dispose of Walden.

Bill Green rode over to Walden's camp one night and took supper. After supper Walden walked out with him to where his horse was tied. Ed Green, who was hiding behind the tent, stepped up and shot him. Marshal Rutherford got word of the killing and sent Ledbetter and Deputy Lon Lewis after the Greens. The marshals scouted the Caney River country for days without finding a trace of them.

A week later, they were on the trail again. The Greens had held up the L.J. Snarr coal works three miles northwest of Oologah, lined up the employees, including Snarr himself, and frisked their pockets. The robbery netted only $28, so they held up two stores at Ringwood and Posey Creek.

The marshals set up camp not far from the Green place and sent word to C.M. McClellan, well-known Indian scout and rancher, that outlaws were on the dodge in the area and often stole horses. McClellan was anxious that they be caught. It was decided to find a man who could join the Greens and set them up for the marshals. McClellan found this man in the person of Leonard Trainor, a former employee wanted for stealing cattle. Trainor agreed to help after McClellan promised to drop the charges.

Trainor went to the Green farm, told the old man the law was "nippin' at his heels" and he wanted to hide out with the boys. The old man knew about his trouble and took him to a place six miles west on Mule Creek.

Trainor's mother lived just across the river. On the evening of October 12, 1896, he suggested to the boys that they take supper at his mother's; afterward he would take them to a pasture on the McClellan ranch where they could get some fresh horses. It was understood between Trainor and the marshals as to the time they would cross the river at the old Ash Hopper ford.

As they approached the ford, Trainor fell behind. This aroused the brothers' suspicions. They ordered him to ride up front. They even put him on Bill Green's horse and made him wear Bill's hat and overcoat. Trainor thought he was a "goner" but there was nothing he could do about it now.

Ledbetter and his posse were concealed behind some logs and would have killed him had it not been for McClellan's sharp eyes. In the bright moonlight he recognized Trainor despite his garb, passing the word down the line. As Ed and Bill Green rode up, the marshals blasted them from their saddles with shotguns. Their bodies were taken to Oologah, laid out in a store building and buried the next day, and Milt Barber went to the penitentiary for his part in starting them on their career of crime.

Action Bud wanted, and action he got. Returning to Muskogee after killing the Greens, he was sent after C.K. Brooks, a Negro charged with ravishing and beating nearly to death a young girl at Hudson on the headwaters of the Neosho. Bud took the train to Vinita and finished his journey on horseback.

Brooks was the employee of a white man named Coombs. Coombs was the father of three motherless daughters, Lulu, 16, Cora, 11, and Ida, a baby of five years. On October 28, he started on a business trip to Coffeyville, Kansas, leaving the children in Brooks' care.

At bedtime the little ones retired together in one room. During the night the Negro went to the house and entered the room where the children were sleeping. This aroused the eldest girl, and she called to her sister, Cora, to light the lamp. At that moment Brooks fell on the bed and seized her. She screamed and tried to shove him away, and he clubbed her into unconsciousness.

Cora, scrambling from bed, caught up the baby and fled from the house into the timber. Brooks went to search for them. Failing to find them, he returned to the bedroom.

Lulu had recovered sufficiently to steal away, but he caught her, half dazed, a few yards from the house. Again he raised his club, striking her across the forehead until the weapon broke into pieces. As she lay half dead and helpless, he accomplished his act.

Meanwhile, little Cora had carried her baby sister to the home of the nearest neighbor, a mile and a half away, through the darkness, clad only in her nightgown and tearing her tender feet on the rough, frozen ground. As the whole community aroused to the terrible facts, Lulu was rushed to a physician, and every able-bodied man and boy scoured the country for Brooks. Had they found him, Ledbetter's services would not have been needed.

Bud picked up his trail at the Moore Gibson home, three miles from Hudson. Gibson related how the Negro had come in the night, borrowed a blanket and asked to sleep in the barn till morning. After breakfast, he had taken the road to Lenapah. From there Bud traced him to Bartlesville. For a week Bud tracked him with the tenacity of a bloodhound, finally overtaking him in the Osage. Brooks was returned to Muskogee, convicted of rape, and hanged on July 1, the first man to die on the gallows of the white man's court in Indian Territory.

Bud brought in scores of other badmen during the latter half of the 1890s. But he always figured the highlight of this period of his career was the capture of Al Jennings and his gang December 6, 1897.

Following a couple of comic opera train holdups over in Oklahoma, this bantam, more or less famous outlaw-attorney-movieman led his wild bunch east into the Northern district. Ledbetter and his posse picked up their trail after they entered the Creek Nation. Bud bottled the bandits at the Spike S ranch south of Tulsa, where they managed to escape after a rattling gun battle, but he trapped the wagon in which they were fleeing to Arkansas a few days later by felling a tree where the trail sloped down a deep cut at the rock crossing on Carr Creek southwest of Bond Switch (present Onapa).

The wagon jolted down the frozen road until the team breasted the barricade and the driver found himself looking into the muzzle of Ledbetter's Winchester. At Bud's command, the remnants of the band tossed out their guns, crawled from under the straw and blankets where they were hiding, and surrendered.

By the turn of the century Muskogee was one of the busiest and most interesting cities in the southwest. William McKinley was President, and attendant with the political turnover of federal office holders in Indian Territory, Leo E. Bennett, former Indian Agent and publisher of the

Muskogee *Phoenix,* succeeded Rutherford as U.S. marshal for the Northern district. Bennett had seen fit to keep most of Rutherford's staff, so old-timers like Ledbetter, Jones and Lewis were still in the saddle.

Muskogee was the permanent headquarters for the Dawes Commission with its several hundred employees, completing the allotment of millions of acres to members of each nation of the Five Tribes and breaking up their national governments. The agreements with these tribes also had provided for segregation from allotment of all townsite acreage and the survey, appraisal and sale of lots in the towns to owners of improvements thereon, and sale by auction to the highest bidder of all surplus lots in the townsite reservation. Despite the fact that, until this time, no legal deed to a tract of land in Indian Territory existed, several substantial brick and stone business structures had been erected and many homes built.

The United States clerk's office was a busy place with a large staff, and the recording offices of the Territory and main office of the United States Indian inspectors added many more employees to the government payroll.

The Union Agency for the Five Tribes was there, and General Pleasant Porter, the Creek leader, had his executive offices and permanent home in Muskogee.

The nerve center of all legal and Indian business in the Nations, it was the most important commercial, financial and industrial establishment. The streets and hotels were jammed daily with Indians, lawyers, real estate speculators, adventurers, confidence men and grafters. Although liquor was prohibited, bootleggers and "uno" (you-know) joints supplied the needs of the thirsty, and everyone was confident of the future —except that a new problem had arisen.

The Creek treaty with the United States following the Civil War had freed all their Negro slaves, and the Dawes agreements provided that they be made citizens with all the rights and privileges of their former owners and masters. They had been duly enrolled by the commission, given allotments of land, and accorded the right to vote and hold office. In fact, these Negroes, or "freedmen," as they were called, dominated the House of Warriors of the Creek Council, and occupied a significant number of seats in the House of Kings. As a further blow to Creek Indian pride, freedmen could sell their allotments at will, while allotments to the Indians were restricted and could be disposed of only after approval by the Department of the Interior. Whites, except inter-married citizens, had no voting or property rights at all.

This unusual political and economic situation precipitated bitter clashes that threatened to burst into a full scale war. The freedmen became so impudent and arrogant that in every home and business firearms were kept within easy reach.

The Marshal's office received a hurry-up call from Boynton to send some United States men to quell a riot. Deputies Al Cottle, E.H. Hubbard and Bud Ledbetter were ordered to go. They wired Boynton officers that they were coming and caught the first train. Cottle, reminiscing about the incident years later, stated: "That wire saying Bud and his boys were on the way put the scare in those Negroes so that when we arrived we rounded up one white and twenty-one blacks for being involved, without firing a shot."

Mass arrests did little to relieve the tension. At Braggs, eighteen miles southeast of Muskogee, there had been racial trouble for a year. One morning in May, 1903, a band of armed blacks rode into town, cut all communication wires, then proceeded to annoy and harass the inhabitants. A man named McBloom stepped from his back door and was fired upon by two Negroes concealed in his corn crib. McBloom dodged back into the house and grabbed his gun. As he did so, he yelled to a boy on the other side of the house that they were going to murder him and to ride for help.

The boy reached Muskogee at noon. By that time the ferrymen on the Arkansas river was reporting he had seen women and children leaving their homes in the bottoms and had heard gunfire. A few minutes later, a Negro woman whipped her team into the city, stating she had seen one man ambushed and six whites killed and many others wounded in a clash with the armed invaders. She was so wildly excited that Bud put little stock in her story, but indications were that the situation was critical.

Ledbetter and six deputies reached the scene by late afternoon. Only one person had been injured, but everyone was carrying a pistol, shotgun or rifle. They made seventeen arrests. McBloom's assailants were convicted and sent to the penitentiary.

In this surcharged atmosphere, Muskogee citizens rechecked their weapons and wondered just how long before hell popped there.

It came on a quiet afternoon in 1905.

Some Negroes moved in and took over a vacant office building on 4th street. When the owner said he wanted $10 a month rent, they told him: "This is Indian Territory an' we don't pay rent here. We're armed to the belt an' ready fo' a real showdown."

The frightened owner rushed to the Marshal's office and told Ledbetter. "All right," Bud said, "I'll go up and look 'em over." He strapped on his .45 Colt's. His Winchester .45 saddle gun was be-

ing repaired, so he picked up a government issue
.32 automatic rifle loaded with steel-jacketed cartridges.

He walked up the street a few blocks and
turned north on 4th. The building was a two-
story affair, with two windows above and two
windows and a door on the ground floor. A big
Negro, naked to the waist and with a six-shooter
in his hand, stood on the porch.

As Bud started toward him, a Negro appeared
in each of the upstairs windows and opened fire.
The same moment a man appeared at each corner of the building, and from them and the black
on the porch came a hail of lead.

With bullets whistling around his ears and
jerking at his trousers, Bud went into action.
Two shots from his Colt's emptied the upper floor
windows. Next he killed the Negro at the left corner of the building, put the one at the right corner out of the fight as fast as he could pull the
trigger, then holstered the empty weapon, shifted the rifle from his left hand to right and began
firing from the hip at the man on the porch.

The rifle belched lead like a machine gun, and
Bud was aiming for the big black's mid-section
less than thirty yards distant. But it was not
until his sixth shot that the Negro finally folded
and crumpled to the floor.

The battle was over. Ledbetter reloaded his .45
and looked around. Seeing no other belligerents
anxious to join the contest, he started back to his
office.

The building owner had spread the word. On
Court street Bud met a mob of townsmen on foot,
horseback, in wagons and buggies and armed
with everything that would shoot.

"Where's the riot? How many are dead? We're
with you, Bud . . . ." they said, breathlessly.

Ledbetter checked the bullet holes in his trousers, and in an even drawl replied: "There ain't no

riot. They're all dead." Then, ever thoughtful, he added: "You fellows better get hold of Charley Moore, the undertaker, and help pick up them remains."

One of the most dramatic tragedies in the history of the Territory had been enacted. Colonel Clarence B. Douglas, editor of the *Phoenix,* knew it was good stuff not only for his own paper but for the metropolitan press north and east, and insisted that Bud come into his office.

"It's a whale of a story," Douglas explained, "and I wanted to get the details first hand."

"Ain't no details," Bud said. "I went up there to see what was going on. Them niggers started shootin' at me, so I just killed 'em."

"How come they didn't hit you?" Douglas asked. "There were five of them. They probably averaged four shots each — twenty in all."

"Well, whenever I shoot I always take a step or two sideways, then I'm not where I was, you see."

"So you just stepped from one side to the other. Well, tell me, Bud, weren't you scared?"

"No."

"Were you excited?"

"No."

"Were you nervous?"

"I ain't never nervous."

"Well you must have had some unusual sensation standing there with five men shooting holes in your britches."

"I don't know about sensation and such," Bud said. Then, as an afterthought: "I was a little fretted."

"*Fretted?* I'll be damned!" exclaimed Douglas. "Tell me, Bud — what fretted you? Maybe I can do something to keep it from happening again."

"Well, you see when I began firing at that porch nigger with that fancy little rifle, I knowed I was hitting him in the belly every shot, and

when he wouldn't fall it fretted me, that's all."
Bud rose to go. "Tell you somethin', Colonel —
never go after a shooting man with one of them
new fangled .32s. Get you hurt if you do. Always
take a .45 — that knocks 'em down and they
don't get up and bother you no more."

With that parting advice, Bud left, still the
coolest and least excited man in Muskogee.

Investigation later by Undertaker Moore
showed he was correct. The porch Negro had a
ring) of bullet holes in his stomach all within
three inches of his navel. Any one of these shots
would eventually have been fatal, but they had
produced little shock on impact and zipped
through the body.

This wasn't the end of race turmoil in Indian
Territory. But never again did such an outbreak
occur in Muskogee. The people felt safe in putting away their firearms and going about their
business so long as Bud was around. And he was
around for many years to come.

With the racial situation under control and
most of the old-time gun slinging outlaws fading
into history, Bud was assigned to clean up the
liquor traffic in preparation for statehood. In the
next two years he and his raiders made such a
record that he was given the title of "Carry Nation" Ledbetter. He destroyed scores of stills, con-
fiscated thousands of gallons of whiskey, and became so adept at detecting packages of liquor
shipped into the district by freight and express,
that bootleggers declared he could smell alcohol
in a box car running past at twenty miles an
hour. Barrels of whiskey and mash were destroyed at the stills, but so much jugged and
bottled liquor and beer was hauled to Muskogee
and smashed against the brick wall of the court
building, that broken glass had to be hauled off
by the wagon load and the area smelled like the
back yard of a brewery.

Even the street urchins developed a game in Bud's honor. It usually was played in an old warehouse where they would collect all kinds of bottles and pretend to secret them as if they were grown men. One boy, who played the role of the marshal, would suddenly pounce upon the bottles, smash them, then the game would be adjourned until a fresh supply could be secured.

When the Twin Territories were joined as a single state in 1907, law enforcement became the responsibility of police departments, sheriffs and constables. For federal purposes, Oklahoma was divided into a Western and Eastern district, and each marshal's force reduced to half a dozen. Their work also dwindled to small cases and routine. Many of the former deputies found jobs with the state or municipalities. In 1908, "Uncle Bud," as Ledbetter was now affectionately called, became Chief of Police of Muskogee. In 1912, he was elected sheriff of Muskogee County.

When his term expired, he bought a house, a cow and some chickens and announced that he was hanging up his guns. But the notion soon passed. The criminal element was about to take over Okmulgee. An officer with judgment and bravery was needed. The city fathers sent for Ledbetter. Within a few weeks, he had the situation in hand.

Back in Muskogee the summer of 1922, he was called upon to head posses of much younger men in their hunt for the slayers of Homer Teaff, deputy sheriff. Many a story was told how he kept up with the best of them, sleeping on the ground at night, braving all kinds of weather, rain and lack of food until the killers were caught.

It was election time and many of his friends wanted him to run again for sheriff. Bud declined. "I'm 73 years old," he said, "and people are getting tired of hearing about me."

"Try it and find out," his friends advised.

Uncle Bud won the August primary in a walk. His Republican opponent in the fall was a World War I veteran.

It was youth against old age. But it was more than old age that gave Ledbetter his overwhelming 3,000 majority. Fearless and courteous, determined and kind — these traits of character had made him the most liked officer in eastern Oklahoma. The confidence and respect the people expressed for him that day made him as proud as when he received his first appointment as a young deputy in Arkansas.

Despite his years, he continued his never-ending war against hijackers, thieves, murderers and moonshiners. This time he served two terms as sheriff — until 1928 and his good common sense told him to retire.

In the autumn of his life he was a familiar and venerated figure on the streets of Muskogee and at semi-annual meetings of the Oklahoma Sheriffs and Peace Officers Association, of which he was a charter member and one of the founders. He celebrated his 84th birthday, December 15, 1936, with friends and relatives in Shamrock and Sapulpa and returned to his son's farm south of Muskogee. A few weeks later he entered the city hospital.

Folks all over Oklahoma followed the newspaper accounts of his fight for life against heart disease. His doctors expressed amazement at the tenactiy of the veteran lawman's struggle. When he died, finally, on July 8, 1937, the whole city turned out to pay its respects to this man who bore the distinction of having been in more than a hundred gun battles and never scratched.

JAMES FRANKLIN "BUD" LEDBETTER.

NATHANIEL REED, alias "Texas Jack" — the first, but not the last Indian Territory desperado into whom Ledbetter's bullets put the fear of God. Paroled from prison, he became an evangelist.

FRANK JONES, United States deputy marshal, who accompanied Ledbetter on several of his expeditions.

AL JENNINGS, Oklahoma's more or less famous train robber-attorney-movieman, was captured with remnants of his gang at a rock crossing on Carr Creek by Ledbetter and posse after a gun battle at the Spike S ranch south of Tulsa.

MUSKOGEE at the turn of the century was one of the busiest and most interesting cities in the southwest. Despite the fact there was not a legal deed to a tract of land in Indian Territory, several substantial brick and stone business structures had been erected and many homes built.

CREEK INDIANS and freedmen receiving their allotments at land office, Muskogee, April 1, 1899.

270

COLONEL CLARENCE B. DOUGLAS, editor of the Muskogee Phoenix.

BOOK 6

"Watch out," was the cry across the Southwest, "here comes Cannonball Green!"

14. Jehu of the Stage Lines

He was never an operator like John Butter-field, who launched the first, longest, roughest, most punishing and nerve-racking stage route west of the Mississippi. Nor did he achieve the fame of Ben Holladay, the Stagecoach King. But he was an adept and one of the unsung heroes in the business.

Starting his stage line as a livery operation in Montana the year General George A. Custer's command was annihilated on the Little Big Horn, it spider-webbed rapidly into a network of more than 1,500 miles across lonely plains and mountains. At the peak of his career, he was running nearly four score vehicles and 1,000 horses. It was the invasion of the railroads in the South-west that stopped him short of becoming a millionaire.

His name was D.R. Green, affectionately known as "Cannonball."

Listen to the jingle,
The rumble and the roar
As she glides along the woodlands,
Through the hills and by the shore.

She's mighty long and handsome,
She's known quite well by all . . . .

Just as the record-breaking feats of Cal S. Bun-yan's most wondrous locomotive on the Ireland, Jerusalem, Australian & Southern Michigan Line inspired these words of the popular folk song representing the epitome of efficiency in early rail transportation, the mountain miner and prairie pioneer waited and listened with the same confidence for the jingle, rumble and roar of Green's rocking, straw and vermillion colored Concord, until over the horizon or down the rough mountain trail lurched the fast running coach, with Green himself swaying on the box and driving furiously like Jehu, son of Hanani.

Legend has it that Cal Bunyan's seven hundred car train went so fast that after it was brought to a dead stop it was still making sixty-five miles an hour. One day Cal said to his engineer, "Give her all the snuss she's got." That was the end of the I.J.A. & S.M. Railroad. The train traveled so fast that the friction melted the steel rails and burned the ties to ashes. When it reached the top of the grade, the engine took off like an airplane, carrying itself and seven hundred cars so far into the stratosphere that for years afterward it was claimed to be rushing through space making overnight jumps between the stars!

Old-time hoboes gave a name to this Flying Dutchman of a train:

> From the great Atlantic Ocean
> To the wild Pacific shore . . . .
> She rolls through East St. Louis
> And she never does it slow.
>
> As she flies through Colorado,
> She gives an awful squall
> They tell her by her whistle—
> The Wabash Cannon Ball.

According to Green, who also enjoyed making exaggerated statements about the speed of his vehicles, his stages were so fast that even time could not keep up with them. In fact, he had painted on the side of his pay wagon a picture of Old Father Time, encumbered with a valise, rushing to catch a Cannonball stage.

Whether performing at the ribbons of a four- or six-horse hitch or transacting business in his office, decorated with paintings of famous persons including a portrait of Abe Lincoln, he was surrounded with an aura of importance and authority. He stood a husky six feet "in his sock feet." He wore a fine broadcloth suit and long jacket or duster, which was always left unbuttoned to reveal a fancy tailored vest, draped with a heavy gold watch chain, and a large diamond pin in a velvet neckscarf. A thick gray beard, receding hairline and heavy brows shadowing deep set eyes lent dignity to his appearance. Strangers, unaware of his occupation, often mistook him for a judge.

His large collection of diamonds revealed the flamboyant part of his character. During his affluent period, he boasted: "Reckon I own more diamonds than are owned, altogether, by all other would-be diamond owners in the West." His adored wife would bedeck herself with elaborate jewelry, much to Cannonball's satisfaction. Together they added considerable glamour to frontier social events.

The first stage run he ever made was from Helena, Montana, to Fort Benton, on the headwaters of the Missouri. In the late 1870s he established his southwest system with connections to Colorado, the Texas panhandle and Santa Fe.

The fixed schedule of his route was one hundred miles a day, no more and no less. Once a driver came in two hours late.

He told Green: "There were no passengers, so I thought I'd let the horses take it easy."

"You're new!" shouted Cannonball, then proceeded to give the man a free lecture on the treatment of horseflesh. "Those horses have been injured more by being allowed to take it easy. In service like this horses must be forced to accustom themselves to one gait and keep it."

Green was a stickler for keeping his timetable. He would lay bets with his passengers that he could change teams quicker than any one of them could light a cigar. He always won, for the harness was equipped with snaps like those on fire harness, and he used to make the change almost without stopping.

"Hold onto your hats!" really meant something to travelers on the Cannonball line. "Tie them on tight," Green admonished as he took up the reins, for others were seldom available in the new settlements. And tight schedules, with dinner and rest stops lasting only ten minutes, did not permit halts for retrieving lost haberdashery.

Six passengers who lost their hats on the first lap of one New Mexcio trip were forced to ride bareheaded for hours under a scorching sun.

Green also experienced his share of the rigors and dangers of the frontier. But he always brought his passenger and cargo through in spite of "hell, storm, flood and Indian arrows."

His first coaches were covered spring wagons with a capacity of four passengers, their baggage, and a few hundred pounds of mail. As the larger and resplendent, egg-shaped Concords came into use, he acquired several of them. It was then possible to get seventeen passengers aboard, and travelers no longer were "marooned" at one of his stations for lack of room.

He decorated the door panels with scenic pictures and frequently the likeness of some contemporary actress was painted on either side of the footboard or driver's seat. The mail-carrying coaches were stamped in gold letters: "U.S. Mail."

All who have left records of travel experiences with western stage drivers agree that they possessed positive and distinct personality traits. Some were labeled "dare-devils" and "madmen," others "jovial idiots." Characterization varied with individual background. Some were farmers, turned coachmen, others plain fighters, gamblers and drinkers. But all were self-confident men once in the box and hold of the reins.

In this position, according to one traveling English merchant, the stage driver was inferior to no one in the Republic. "Even the President, were he on board, must submit to his higher authority."

As was customary with most drivers, Cannonball allowed his more distinguished passengers to share the box and indulge in good-humored conversation. One such privileged traveler credited him not only with "great skill and judgment" in managing his teams, but considerable intelligence as well. "In short," he wrote, "he is a living encyclopedia of the country, its conditions and development."

Green's most plush vehicle was his pay coach, which he kept for private use. General Manager Kinsley of the Santa Fe railroad was making a trip over the line. When he reached Kingman, Kansas, Green informed him that his private coach was about to start in the direction he was going and invited Kinsley to accompany him. A "runner" had been sent ahead to announce his coming, and the coach had been equipped with an ice chest stocked with cold bottles.

The Cannonball stage owner and the railroad executive had traveled a long time over the desert.

"It's hot," suggested Cannonball.

Kinsley assented.

"Thirsty?" inquired the owner of the stage line.

The railroad man's mouth was parched.

A short time afterward Green received a letter from the Santa Fe stating that the company was sending a new private car to California, and asked if he would like to occupy it. He accepted the invitation, and needless to say the car was one of the most plush on the line and well-stocked with cold bottles. As he was winding up his Pacific Coast visit, Green received another letter from the railroad stating that it was about to send a private car back as far as Topeka, and inquired if he happened to be going that direction. It was the railroad's way of returning the courtesy Cannonball had shown its official.

In the early 1880s, Green moved his headquarters to Kingman, then terminus of the railroad for all westbound mail, passengers and settlers seeking claims in this highly publicized "Garden of Eden." He opened a new route 100 miles west to Coldwater — a ten-hour run across favorable terrain in good weather.

The venture proved highly successful. He soon was making three round trips a week, while the hacks of his competitors stood idle and travelers sought his fine coaches and genial manner. He even gave "windjamers" (newspaper reporters) and men of importance free passes to say a good word for his line.

He answered settlers' questions about this strange but beautiful land, rolling as far as the eye could see and carpeted with lush, natural grasses. He helped them select locations for homes near wood and water, and discussed in detail the advantages and disadvantages of a sod shanty, dugout and half-dugout.

Green found a choice location himself near Medicine River, north of Coldwater, where he built his prairie mansion, named "Fairlawn." He filled the house with expensive furniture and bric-a-brac and lived there with his family in grand Southern style, complete with Negro maids and servants.

The demand for his service grew. Surrounding towns requested routes connecting with the end of track. Pratt, Kansas, offered a Main Street lot and barn for his coaches. Wellsford offered twenty acres adjoining the town. Leoti offered eight

Main Street lots. Meade a lot fronting the square and $500, and Garden City six lots and $1,000.

"I'll come for six lots in each town and $1,000," Green replied, and the towns accepted.

He made his first trip with great ostentation, and the shortest time ever attained by stage between Coldwater and Garden City. In the center of town his coach wheel caught a truck gardener's cart and scattered cabbages, pumpkins and every other kind of vegetable over the street. An angry German rushed out and demanded damages.

Green was wearing plenty of diamonds. He waited until the crowd was sufficiently large, then inquired the amount. The German thought that $25 would do. Green took from his pocket a roll of bills with a $500 wrapper, smilingly peeled off a $100 note and flung it to the gardener. Cannonball was solid forever with his patrons.

His network of routes expanded so rapidly the next three years that he was forced to give up stage driving and travel about in his colorful pay wagon, checking each station once a month.

During his trips he had an opportunity to observe Jacob Barney, a Kansas pioneer, lay out the town of Janesville to the north and wade through the seemingly endless government red tape acquiring a post office. He also noted that quick, easy money was being made laying out towns in advance of westward migration.

Janesville lay in Section 18 of Edwards County. Under Kansas law, sections 16 and 36 were declared state school land. Title to these could be obtained in half the time necessary to gain title to other sections. By an act of the Kansas legislature March 5, 1875, Kiowa County had been abolished and the territory divided between Edwards and Comanche counties.

Cannonball induced a group of Kingman

281

friends to form a town company. Early in 1885, he laid out a new townsite in Section 16, little more than a mile east of Janesville. The new town was named Greensburg, in his honor.

In less than four months it had 1,000 inhabitants and nearly a dozen brick and stone buildings. What Greensburg needed was a post office.

Cannonball had no patience for government red tape. He went to the citizens of Janesville with the proposition that by moving to Section 16 they could prove their claims in six months. Most of the residents moved at once. On a dark night in November, the founding fathers quietly went to Janesville, loaded the post office on a sled with the postmaster asleep therein, and dragged the building to Greensburg. The populace was delighted to find it open and ready for business next morning.

Cannonball then led a movement to re-form Kiowa County. The request was granted. Governor John A. Martin appointed a census taker in February, 1886. The returns made on March 19 showed a population of 2,704, of whom 549 were householders, and $236,622 worth of taxable property. On March 23, Governor Martin issued a proclamation of organization, and named Greensburg the county seat.

Greensburg brought lasting fame to Cannonball. It was also the beginning of the end of his stage operations.

In 1886 three railroads — the Atchison, Topeka & Santa Fe, the St. Louis — San Francisco and the Chicago, Rock Island & Pacific — made propositions to the people of the country. The proposition to issue bonds for the first was defeated, and the A.T. & S.F. changed its route. The Chicago, Rock Island & Pacific built a line from Hutchinson through the county. Later, the Atchison, Topeka & Santa Fe built a line across the southeast corner.

Slowly the iron horse chewed up Green's stage line. To add to his dilemma the settlers suffered their first big crop failure from drought. Green was forced to abandon his routes to Leoti and Garden City.

In August 1887, he suffered his second great financial loss. His huge barn at Fairlawn burned, destroying sixty-five tons of millet, oat and hay. Only his horses were saved.

These misfortunes were soon forgotten. In 1888, he was elected to represent Kiowa County in the state legislature.

Cannonball viewed this honor as the first step to an important new career, which ended as quickly as it started. During the legislative session at Topeka the spring of 1889, he locked horns with Senator Joseph R. Burton, who was serving his third term and a power in corporation affairs.

According to one account, Green was speaking in his stentorian voice and Burton suggested that he step out in the aisle so the galleries could hear him better. Green retorted:

"If the Senator can't hear me, he should take a match and clean the ___ out of his ears."

The senator was miffed. When someone asked, "Who is he?" Burton quipped: "He's a Jehu called Cannonball, who runs some kind of stage line."

During the remainder of the session, Cannonball was referred to as "Jehu" Green.

He was still in Topeka on March 23 when President Benjamin Harrison issued his proclamation opening the Unassigned Lands in Indian Territory to settlement at 12 o'clock noon, April 22. Kansas homeseekers headed for the area on horseback, afoot and in every kind of conveyance. Others poured into Arkansas City, where the Santa Fe amassed much passenger equipment and ran it in 12-car trains with a total of 10,000 passengers to where U.S. troops guarded the borders.

The Chicago, Kansas & Nebraska, a branch of the Rock Island, had been building down the Chisholm Trail from Caldwell, Kansas, toward Fort Reno, in the southeastern corner of the Cheyenne-Arapaho reservation. Due to financial difficulties it had reached only as far as Pond Creek, in the Cherokee Outlet, thirty-six miles short of the Unassigned Lands.

President March Low, of the C.J.&N. wanted in on the gravy. He summoned Cannonball into his Topeka office. "If you will run your stages from the end of track down the 'Reno Road' into this territory, we will attach a stage ticket to our train ticket at $6 per head."

Green snapped up the offer. Within two weeks he had assembled every coach, wagon and buggy and pulled every experienced driver he could spare from his entire network. The vehicles and drivers were rushed to Pond Creek via the Rock Island, and relays of fresh horses were posted at ten-mile intervals. When the great mass of humanity surged forward to the crack of carbines and call of bugles, Cannonball rolled his equipment. It is claimed that not a single enthusiastic land-seeker who chose his transportation that immortal day failed to reach a claim safely and in good time.

Green received additional compensation for a job well done. The C.K.&N. contracted with him to operate a stage line to Fort Reno "pending completion of its track." It took up some of the slack created by the loss of service to Leoti and Garden City.

Back in Kansas, however, things were not rosy. The sudden exodus of residents to the Oklahoma country had virtually depleted many towns. Greensburg had shrunk to less than a third of its population. Property values went down. And Cannonball failed in his bid for re-election to the state legislature. Steel rails finger-ing throughout the country made stage transpor-tation obsolete. Then came the nationwide de-pression of 1892. Green sold his diamonds and other possessions piecemeal to feed his family.

In 1893, he made the "run" into the Cherokee Outlet, obtaining a claim three miles northwest of Pond Creek, and moved his family to Oklaho-ma. Down to his "last milch cow and a pair of mules," he again turned to politics, and was elected first treasurer of Grant County. He made only a meager living. There was no opportunity to recapture his fortune.

When the Kiowa-Comanche country, Oklaho-ma's last frontier, opened in 1901, he went to Caddo County and secured a farm near Bridge-port on the South Canadian, fertile enough to provide a livelihood for his two sons.

At age 64 he did little except look after his new claim. Still active in politics, he became one of more than 1,000 territorial delegates who attend-ed the "monster" convention at Delmar Gardens in Oklahoma City on July 12, 1905, to petition the 59th Congress to favorably consider Oklaho-ma for statehood.

During this convention Green struck up a friendship with Oklahoma's last territorial governor, Frank Frantz. Frantz knew of Green's record in Kansas and that his brother for years had been the attorney general of California. Frantz found a job for the old stage driver. For the next two years, Cannonball traveled over various counties, inspecting the condition of school lands leased to farmers and determining whether the rent should be increased.

When he was 70, his attorney general brother persuaded him to come to California "to escape the severe winters." He settled in Long Beach, became active in community affairs, and served one term on the city council.

A staging contest was being held at the Sacramento fair. Cannonball still boasted of his proficiency with the ribbons. There were many entries. The express companies came up with fine teams and coaches; railroad companies entered teams and drivers who had operated in connection with their various lines.

Cannonball appeared with an old Overland coach and a six-horse bronco team covered with red mountain dust. After all the drivers had exhibited their best stunts, he cut a figure eight with his outfit around the judges stand in such a manner that even the old-timers present held their breath. He carried away the honors and the hearts of a cheering, admiring crowd.

He died at Long Beach in 1922 at age 85 — Jehu of the stage lines to the last.

D.R. "CANNONBALL" GREEN. Strangers often mistook him for a judge.

BIBLIOGRAPHY

ABE LINCOLN OF THE DELAWARES

Battey, Thomas C. *The Life and Adventures of A Quaker Among the Indians.* Lee and Shepard, Publishers, Boston — Lee, Shepard and Dillingham, New York, 1875.

Brown, D. Alexander. "Black Beaver." *American History Illustrated,* Vol. II, No. 2, May, 1967.

Connelley, William E. *A Standard History of Kansas and Kansans,* Vol. I. Lewis Publishing Company, Chicago and New York, 1918.

Dodge, Colonel Richard Irving. *Our Wild Indians.* A.D. Worthington and Company, Hartford, Conn., 1882.

Foreman, Carolyn Thomas. "Black Beaver." *Chronicles of Oklahoma,* Vol. XXIV, No. 3, Autumn, 1946.

Foreman, Grant. *Advancing the Frontier, 1830-1860.* University of Oklahoma Press, Norman, 1933.

_____ (Editor). *Adventure on Red River.* University of Oklahoma Press, Norman, 1937.

_____ . *Marcy and the Gold Seekers.* University of Oklahoma Press, Norman, 1939.

Marcy, Randolph B. *The Prairie Traveler, A Handbook for Overland Expeditions.* Harper and Brothers, Publishers, New York, 1859.

_____ . *Thirty Years of Army Life on the Border.* Harper and Brothers, Publishers, New York, 1866.

McCracken, H.L. "The Delaware Big House." *Chronicles of Oklahoma,* Vol. XXXIV, No. 2, Summer, 1956.

Nicholson, William. "A Tour of Indian Agencies in Kansas and the Indian Territory in 1870." *Kansas Historical Quarterly,* Vol. II, No. 4, November, 1934.

Ridings, Sam P. *The Chisholm Trail.* Co-Operative Publishing Company, Guthrie, Oklahoma, 1936.

Tatum, Lawrie. *Our Red Brothers and the Peace Policy of President Ulysses S. Grant.* University of Nebraska Press, Lincoln, 1970.

Wellman, Paul I. *The Trampling Herd.* J.B. Lippincott Company, Philadelphia and New York, 1931.

BARD OF THE OKTAHUTCHEE

Challacombe, Doris. "Alexander Lawrence Posey." *Chronicles of Oklahoma,* Vol. XI, No. 4, December, 1933.

Dale, Edward Everett. "The Journal of Alexander Lawrence Posey, January 1 to September 4, 1897." *Chronicles of Oklahoma,* Vol.XLV, No. 4, Winter, 1967-68.

Hall, George Riley. "Alexander Posey, Indian Poet of the Transition, Was Sensitive Lover of Nature." *Daily Oklahoman,* April 23, 1939.

———. "The Old Council House." *Chronicles of Oklahoma,* Vol. XIII, No. 2, June, 1935.

Meserve, John Bartlett. "The Plea of Crazy Snake." *Chronicles of Oklahoma,* Vol. XI, No. 3, September, 1933.

McRill, Leslie A. "One Hundred Years of Oklahoma Verse, 1830-1930." *Chronicles of Oklahoma,* Vol. XXXIII, No. 1, Spring, 1955.

Posey, Alexander Lawrence. "Hotgun on the Death of Yadeka Harjo." *Sturm's Oklahoma Magazine,* Vol. VI, No. 3, May, 1908.

———. "Journal of Creek Enrollment Field Party 1905." *Chronicles of Oklahoma,* Vol. XLVI, No. 1, Spring, 1968.

Posey, Mrs. Minnie H. and Connelley, William Elsey. *The Poems of Alexander Posey.* Crane and Company, Topeka, 1910.

Thoburn, Joseph A. *A Standard History of*

Oklahoma, Vol. II. The American Historical Society, Chicago and New York, 1916.

(Correspondence and contemporary clippings. In author's collection.)

ROUGH RIDER OF THE PAWNEES

El Reno News, May 13, 1898.

Finney, Frank F. "William Pollock: Pawnee Indian, Artist and Rough Rider." *Chronicles of Oklahoma,* Vol. XXXIII, No. 4, Winter, 1955-56.

Kansas City Star, March 24, 1899.

Oklahoma State Capital, March-November, 1899.

Pawnee Times-Democrat, March-November, 1899.

Roosevelt, Theodore. "The Rough Riders." *Scribner's Magazine,* Vol. XXV, Nos. 1-4, January-April, 1899.

(Interviews and correspondence. In author's collection.)

BAREHANDED BULLFIGHTER

"Bill Pickett, First Bulldogger." *Ebony,* Vol. XV, No. 10, August, 1960.

Clancy, Foghorn. *My Fifty Years in Rodeo, Living With Cowboys, Horses and Danger.* The Naylor Company, San Antonio, 1952.

Collings, Ellsworth and England, Alma Miller. *The 101 Ranch.* University of Oklahoma Press, Norman, 1937.

Day, Beth. *America's First Cowgirl, Lucille Mulhall.* Julian Messner, Inc., New York, 1955.

Gipson, Fred. *Fabulous Empire, Colonel Zack Miller's Story.* Houghton Mifflin Company, Boston, 1955.

Hinkle, Milt. "Bulldoggers!" *True West,* Vol. 14, No. 2, November-December, 1967.

_____. "The Dusky Demon." *True West,* Vol. 8, No. 6, July-August, 1961.

_____. "Spradley of the 101." *True West,* Vol. 12, No. 1, September-October, 1964.

Howard, Robert West and Arnold, Oren. *Rodeo, Last Frontier of the Old West.* New American Library, New York, 1961.

O'Brien, Esse Forrester. *The First Bulldogger.* The Naylor Company, San Antonio, 1961.

Thompson, W.C. "Hand to Horn Battle With An Enraged Bull." *New York Herald Co.,* 1910.

(Interviews, correspondence, contemporary clippings, and 101 Ranch Wild West show pamphlets and memorabilia. In author's collection.)

LASSO GENIUS

Byers, Chester. With contributions by Fred Stone, Will Rogers and Elsie Janis. *Roping, Trick and Fancy Rope Spinning.* G.P. Putnam's Sons, New York, 1928.

Rogers, Betty. *Will Rogers, His Wife's Story.* The Bobbs-Merrill Company, Indianapolis and New York, 1941.

Shirley, Glenn. *Pawnee Bill, A Biography of Major Gordon W. Lillie.* The University of New Mexico Press, Albuquerque, 1957.

(Interviews, correspondence, contemporary clippings, and Pawnee Bill Wild West show records, together with written memoirs of Mrs. Effie Barrera, 1941. In author's collection.)

PINT-SIZED BRONC TWISTER

McGinty, Billy. *The Old West.* The Ripley Review, Publishers, 1937.

(Reminiscences of Billy McGinty, dictated at Ripley, Oklahoma, 1957-1958, together with letters, documents, contemporary clippings and photographs. In author's collection.)

PRINCESS WENONA

Havinghurst, Walter. *Annie Oakley of the Wild West.* The MacMillan Company, New York, 1954.

Russell, Don. *The Lives and Legends of Buffalo Bill.* University of Oklahoma Press, Norman, 1960.

_____. *The Wild West, or, A History of the Wild West Shows.* Amon Carter Museum of Western Art, 1970.

(Contemporary clippings and Buffalo Bill, Pawnee Bill and 101 Ranch Wild West show pamphlets and memorabilia. In author's collection.)

WOMAN OF DESTINY

Anonymous. "The Recrudescence of Kate Barnard." *Harlow's Weekly,* Vol. 22, No. 20, May 19, 1923.

Barnard Collection, Oklahoma Historical Society.

Barnard, Kate. "Address." International Congress on Tuberculosis, Washington, 1908.

_____. "Human Ideals in Government." *The Survey,* Vol. XXIII, October 2, 1909.

_____. "References to Her Life Work." Typescript of notes and sketches compiled by Miss Barnard to use in her early history of Oklahoma and autobiography. (Edith Copeland Personal Papers, Norman, Oklahoma.)

_____. "Shaping the Destinies of the New State." *Proceedings of the National Conference of Charities and Corrections, 1908.* Edited by Alexander Johnson. Fort Wayne: Press of Fort Wayne Printing Co., 1908.

_____. "The New State and Its Children." *Proceedings of the Fourth Annual Meeting of the National Child Labor Committee.* Philadelphia:

The American Academy of Political and Social Science, 1908.

_____. "Through the Windows of Destiny; How I Visualized My Life Work." *Good Housekeeping,* Vol. LV, November, 1912.

_____. "Working for the Friendless." *The Independent,* Vol. LXIII, November 28, 1907.

Bennett, Helen Christine. *American Women in Civic Work.* Dodd, Mead and Company, 1915.

Ellis, Albert H. *A History of the Constitutional Convention of the State of Oklahoma.* Muskogee: Economy Printing Company, 1923.

First Annual Report of the Department of Charities and Corrections for the Year 1908. Guthrie: The Leader Printing Company, 1908.

Hurst, Irvin. *The 46th Star.* Semco Color Press, Inc., Oklahoma City, 1957.

Journal of the Council Proceedings of the Eighth Legislative Assembly of the Territory of Oklahoma, January 10-March 10, 1905. Guthrie, O.T.: The State Capital Company, 1905.

"Kate Barnard." *The National Cyclopaedia of American Biography,* Vol. XV. James T. White & Company, New York, 1916.

M'Kiddy, J.H. "Kate Barnard, Unsung Heroine." *Daily Oklahoman,* February 23, 1941.

McKelway, A.J. " 'Kate,' the 'Good Angel' of Oklahoma." *American Magazine,* Vol. LXVI, October, 1908.

" 'Miss Kate,' Livest Wire In Prison Reform, Visits Us." *New York Times,* Magazine Section, Part Six, December 8, 1912.

Murray, William H. "The Constitutional Convention." *Chronicles of Oklahoma,* Vol. IX, No. 2, June, 1931.

Second Annual Report of the Commissioner of Charities and Corrections from October 1, 1909 to October 1, 1910. Oklahoma City: Warden Printing Company, 1910.

(Contemporary clippings, 1906-1930. In

author's collection.)

THE RAVAGING BUCKS

Buck et. al. v. United States, 163 U.S. 678, March, 1896.

Harman, S.W. *Hell on the Border: He Hanged Eighty-Eight Men.* (Compiled by C.P. Sterns.) The Phoenix Publishing Company, Ft. Smith, Arkansas, 1898.

Harrington, Fred Harvey. *Hanging Judge.* The Caxton Printers, Ltd., Caldwell, Idaho, 1951.

Interview with Alec Berryhill, June 28, 1937. *Indian-Pioneer History,* Vol. 14, pp. 478-482, Oklahoma Historical Society.

Interview with Benton Callahan, August 27, 1937. *Indian-Pioneer History,* Vol. 18, pp. 139-144, Oklahoma Historical Society.

Jones, W.F. *The Experiences of A Deputy U.S. Marshal of the Indian Territory,* n.p., 1937.

Records of the United States District Court for the Western District of Arkansas, 1895-1896.

Shirley, Glenn. *Law West of Fort Smith. A History of Frontier Justice in the Indian Territory 1834-1896.* Henry Holt and Company, New York, 1957.

(Correspondence and contemporary clippings. In author's collection.)

MAD ARTIST OF McALESTER

"Convict-Artist Will Pay Full Penalty." *Muskogee Daily Phoenix,* May 6, 1934.

El Reno News, April 23, 1897; December 9-16, 1898.

In the matter of the application of Louis Maas, as Guardian of Conrad Maas, for a writ of Habeas Corpus (June 30, 1900). 10 Oklahoma Reports 302-307.

Oklahoma City Times, April 6, 1936; November 8, 1957.

Oklahoma State Capital, December 20, 1898; October 14, 1899; November 9, 1899; June 23-28, 1906; July 21-22, 1906; June 29, 1907.

Records of Oklahoma State Penitentiary, McAlester, Oklahoma.

Watonga Republican, December, 1898; January-February, 1899.

QUAKER MARSHAL

Barde, Frederick S. (Compiled by). *Life and Adventures of "Billy" Dixon, of Adobe Walls,* Texas Panhandle. Co-Operative Publishing Company, Guthrie, Oklahoma, 1914.

Collins, Hubert E. "Ben Williams, Frontier Peace Officer." Chronicles of Oklahoma, Vol. X, No. 4, December, 1932.

_____. *Warpath and Cattle Trail.* William Morrow and Company, New York, 1928.

Grinnell, George Bird. *The Fighting Cheyennes.* Charles Scribner's Sons, New York, 1915.

Meredith, Grace E. (Revised and Edited by). *Girl Captives of the Cheyennes, A True Story of the Capture and Rescue of Four Pioneer Girls.* Gem Publishing Company, Los Angeles, 1927.

Miles, Nelson A. *Personal Recollections and Observations of General Nelson A. Miles.* The Werner Company, Chicago and New York, 1896.

Ridings, Sam P. *The Chisholm Trail.* Co-Operative Publishing Company, Guthrie, Oklahoma, 1936.

PEACEMAKER OF THE OSAGE

Hill, Luther B. *A History of the State of Oklahoma,* Vol. II. Lewis Publishing Company, Chicago and New York, 1909.

In the Matter of the Identification of the

Bodies of William Martin and Sam Martin. Testimony taken in the office of the United States Marshal at Guthrie, Oklahoma Territory, before George M. Green, United States Commissioner, on August 11, 1903.

Records of U.S. Department of the Interior, United States Indian Service, July, 1899 to October, 1915.

United States v. William Martin, alias Rube Stanley, Sam Martin, alias Sam Stanley, and William H. Smith, alias Indian Bill Smith. Case No. 39185-D, United States District Court, District of Colorado, Denver, June, 1903.

(Correspondence, documents, contemporary clippings and photographs. In author's collection.)

"CARRY NATION" LAWMAN

Benedict, John D. *Muskogee and Northeastern Oklahoma,* Vol. II. The S.J. Clarke Publishing Company, Chicago, 1922.

"Bud Ledbetter, Famous Early Bandit Fighter, Not Too Old To Be Sheriff, Voters Think." *Muskogee Daily Phoenix,* November 11, 1922.

Douglas, Colonel Clarence B. "Bud Ledbetter's One-Man Race Riot." *Daily Oklahoman,* 1936.

Herman, S.W. *Hell on the Border: He Hanged Eighty-Eight Men.* (Compiled by C.P. Sterns.) The Phoenix Publishing Company, Ft. Smith, Arkansas, 1898.

McKennon, C.H. *Iron Men.* Doubleday & Company, Inc., Garden City, New York, 1967.

———. "On the Side of the Law." *Tulsa World,* November 5, 1961.

Nix, Evett Dumas. *Oklahombres.* Eden Publishing House, St. Louis & Chicago, 1929.

"Noted Outlaw Catcher, 'Bud' Ledbetter, Has Had Many Thrilling Experiences in the Indian Territory." *Muskogee Phoenix,* March 28, 1908.

Stansbery, Lon R. "Bud Ledbetter—Scourge of Criminals." *Tulsa World,* January 24, 1937.

_____ . *The Passing of 3D Ranch.* George W. Henry Printing Co., Tulsa, Oklahoma, n.d.

Starr, Helen and Hill, O.E. *Footprints in the Indian Nation.* Hoffman Printing Co., Inc., Muskogee, Oklahoma, 1974.

West, C.W. "Dub". *Persons and Places in Indian Territory.* Muskogee Publishing Company, Muskogee, Oklahoma, 1974.

(Interviews, correspondence and contemporary clippings. In author's collection.)

JEHU OF THE STAGE LINES

Banning, Captain William and George Hugh. *Six Horses.* The Century Company, New York and London, 1930.

Blackmar, Frank W. (Editor). *Kansas, A Cyclopedia of State History,* Vol. II. Standard Publishing Company, Chicago, 1912.

Bredlow, Thomas G. "Stagecoach!" *Frontier Times,* Vol. 34, No. 3, Summer, 1960.

"Cannonball Green, Driver." *Oklahoma State Capital,* October 14, 1906.

"Cannonball Green, Famous Stage Driver, Might Have Been A Millionaire." *Oklahoma State Capital,* March 22, 1908.

Frizzell, John and Mildred. "Cannon Ball Green." *Frontier Times,* Vol. 42, No. 4, June-July, 1968.

Moody, Ralph. *Stagecoach West.* Thomas Y. Crowell Company, New York, 1967.

Winther, Oscar Osburn. *The Transportation Frontier, Trans-Mississippi West, 1865-1890.* Holt, Rinehart and Winston, New York, 1964.